Portrait of God

BRIDGES Youth Series

Kevin Stiffler,
Editor and Publisher

Mary Jaracz and
Virginia L. Wachenschwanz,
Layout and Design

Published quarterly for the teaching church by Warner Press, Inc., 1201 East Fifth Street, Anderson, Indiana 46012. Printed in the United States of America. For information, contact: Warner Press Inc, PO Box 2499, Anderson, Indiana 46018-2499. Lessons based on International Sunday School lessons: the International Bible Lessons for Christian Teaching. Copyright © 1971 by Committee on Uniform Series. Scripture taken from the HOLY BIBLE, NEW INTERNATIONAL VERSION NIV®. Copyright © 2006, 2012 by International Bible Society. Used by permission of Zondervan Publishing House. All rights reserved.

ISBN: 978-1-59317-575-7

Warner Press
Copyright © Warner Press, Inc.

Conte

MW00974750

SESSION   TITLE

Unit I

March

Unit II

April

Unit III

May

About this Book

Embracing Technology

In the early days of the Church of God, they had this thing they called the "Floating Bethel." It was a barge on the Ohio River. They built a chapel on it and evangelized along the river at every landing. Over in England they had this thing called the "Gospel Van," an enclosed wagon that displayed literature but also provided living quarters for the missionary personnel and cooking facilities to feed the hungry. At the end of the 19th century, these ventures were on the cutting edge of technology.

Technology has improved over the years—and it has become much more accessible to many more people. I shudder to think of the work that I had to do for my high school writing assignments—hand-written in ink. No Internet for research. No computer for typing, saving, spell-checking, and printing. I'm sure I have some of those papers saved somewhere. To look at them now, their age would be blatantly obvious. And to show you curriculum or printed Bible study materials from even ten years ago, there would be a noticeable difference.

Paul's words about becoming all things to all people in order to save some (1 Corinthians 9:22) are good advice. Utilizing new technologies in order to save some is not too bad, either.

Keep in touch and keep up the good work!

Kevin Stiffler, Editor and Publisher

Portable Sanctuary

The **Portable Sanctuary** is designed to be copied and distributed to students at the end of each week's session. This handout will continue the ideas from the session throughout the week with additional scripture references, stories, journaling, and prayer topics. This will give students an opportunity to establish some daily devotional time that builds on a consistent theme.

Encourage students to use the Portable Sanctuary, and lead them in this effort by using it yourself. Allow time at the beginning of each session to review last week's Portable Sanctuary and have some extra copies available for any students who were not present last week.

Digital Bridges is an interactive CD-ROM available for purchase to supplement this printed book.

From quarter to quarter Digital Bridges contains different things such as a video introduction to the book, teaching tips, videos, songs (that will also play with just a CD player), interactive games, projection sheets, color pictures and slide presentations, links to some great websites, and all of the printed curriculum in PDF format for you to customize and print at your convenience. These features can be used in preparation for and during your time in the classroom to enhance the teaching and learning experience.

Whenever you see (DB) in the book, it indicates a place where Digital Bridges can be used.

Authors

U N I T 1

Christ, the Image of God
Sharon Bernhardt lives in Penang, Malaysia, with her husband and three sons, where she serves as a schoolteacher. She has written frequently for BRIDGES and *Pathways to God*.

U N I T 2

Christ Sustains and Supports
Keah (Kendall) Redder has served as a youth pastor in Exeter, California, and studied at Mars Hill Graduate School in Seattle, Washington. She currently lives in Fort Collins, Colorado, where she gets paid to hang out with junior high kids at a local school choir program. When not pounding the ivories, Keah dreams of moving to the mountains and becoming a professional ski bum. Then she wakes up and realizes how silly that sounds ... or does it?

U N I T 3

Christ Guides and Protects
Randy Archer pastors the Lents-Gilbert Church of God in Portland, Oregon, where he lives with his wife Alisha, sons Cody and Ethan, and daughter Julia. Raised on the West Coast, a graduate of Azusa Pacific University, he enjoys the incredible roller coaster ride of journeying with Christ. Randy loves being with family, surfing, good music, and great coffee.

Bible Background was written by Merle D. Strege, professor of historical theology at Anderson University.

Mentoring—The Key Ingredient*

As I think about leadership and life, I think about those who really make a difference and experience life to the fullest. They almost always have strong positive mentor figures in their lives. All of us have mentors, whether we want them or not. Parents often set the tone of how we view life and how we react to situations. Our peers, teachers, and coaches growing up are types of mentors. Some of these models are positive and some of these move us to unhealthy patterns. Yet, research shows that most teenagers (and I believe adults, also) who stick with their faith have strong positive mentors in their lives.

Creating a mentoring culture in your youth ministry—where students are being intentionally mentored by older leaders, having peer-to-peer accountability, and also mentoring someone younger than they are—is vitally important. This should also apply to us as leaders. It is critical to find this same design: above (older/wiser), peer-to-peer, and younger.

We often spend a lot of time on programming, but not a lot of time matching up mentors with our students or teaching them how to mentor. Students often won't remember the details about your programs when they leave your ministry, but they will remember someone who cared and poured into them.

Often it is hard to find our own mentors for our lives as youth leaders. Check out www.lead222.com for help on free coaching. Mentoring should be a key focus in your life and your ministry. It makes a difference.

* Adapted from http://www.jesusisthesubject.org/files/downloads/documents/ymi/ymi0915.htm, as accessed on November 10, 2015.

UNIT ONE

INTRO

Christ, the Image of God

CHRIST, THE IMAGE OF GOD

It's the greatest mystery of all time: how could God, Creator of the universe, come to earth in human form? It's something that is difficult to comprehend and impossible to scientifically explain. The Scriptures describe Christ as God's Son, who came to redeem humankind from sin. The coming of Christ—his Advent—is therefore cause for great celebration and awe, an incredible mystery, full of love.

Session 1 will explore the supremacy of Christ, "double agent" of heaven and earth. Session 2 will look at Christ's reflection of God's glory and being. Session 3 will examine the light of God that shines in our lives through Jesus Christ. Session 4 will study the incarnation of the Word of God in Christ. Session 5 will focus on the humility of Christ—an attitude that each of us should have.

What incredible love God has for us that he would step into our shoes!

Unit 1 Special Prep

SESSION 1—WARM UP, Option 2 (More Prep), requires a picture, video clip, model, and real example of a car, and DVD player; you can also use the Digital BRIDGES CD and a computer. STARTING LINE, Option 1 (Younger Youth), calls for water, ice, and steam. For STARTING LINE, Option 2 (Older Youth), you can use clay, playdough, or other props, and prizes. For STRAIGHT AWAY you can use butcher paper and markers. FINISH LINE, Option 2 (More Prep), requires a spinner from a game and a board with corresponding questions.

SESSION 2—For WARM UP, Option 1 (Little Prep), you can use one main prize and some smaller prizes. WARM UP, Option 2 (More Prep), calls for leaves, textured objects, crayons, scissors, and tape. STARTING LINE, Option 1 (Younger Youth), requires pictures of "firstborns." STARTING LINE, Option 2 (Older Youth), calls for a mirror, chairs, a barrier, and an outside volunteer. HOME STRETCH, Option 1 (Younger Youth), requires cardstock paper, scissors, markers, and zip-lock plastic bags. For HOME STRETCH, Option 2 (Older Youth), you can use background music. FINISH LINE, Option 2 (More Prep), calls for guests of other faiths to visit your class.

SESSION 3—WARM UP, Option 1 (Little Prep), requires a dark space and a light source. WARM UP, Option 2 (More Prep), calls for a person who is blind to visit your class. STARTING LINE, Option 1 (Younger Youth), requires chairs, buckets, cotton balls, a serving spoon, and a blindfold. For STARTING LINE, Option 2 (Older Youth), you can use the Digital BRIDGES CD, a computer, and a data projector. HOME STRETCH, Option 2 (Older Youth), calls for candles and matches; you can also use the Digital BRIDGES CD, a computer, and a data projector. FINISH LINE, Option 2 (More Prep), requires candle-making materials, wicks, ribbon, a hole punch, and paper tags.

SESSION 4—WARM UP, Option 1 (Little Prep), calls for index cards. WARM UP, Option 2 (More Prep), requires magazines, markers, poster board, scissors, and glue. HOME STRETCH, Option 1 (Younger Youth), calls for paper hearts, string or yarn, a hole punch, and markers. For HOME STRETCH, Option 2 (Older Youth), you can use the Digital BRIDGES CD, a computer, and a data projector. FINISH LINE, Option 2 (More Prep), requires supplies for making tie-dyed T-shirts.

SESSION 5—WARM UP, Option 2 (More Prep), calls for access to a copy machine. STARTING LINE, Option 1 (Younger Youth), requires magazines, scissors, glue, and markers. HOME STRETCH, Option 2 (Older Youth), calls for towels, basins of water, tubs, and a basket. FINISH LINE, Option 2 (More Prep), requires service project ideas; you can also make "kindness" cards.

Leading into the Session

Warm Up

Option 1 Consider the roles we fulfill.
LITTLE PREP   *Paper, pens or pencils*
Option 2 Discuss different representations.
MORE PREP   *Picture, video clip, model, and real example of a car; DVD player; Digital BRIDGES CD and computer (optional)*

Starting Line

Option 1 Look at different forms.
YOUNGER YOUTH   *Water, ice, steam, chalkboard or dry erase board*
Option 2 Perform some proverbs.
OLDER YOUTH   *Reproducible 1, chalkboard or dry erase board; paper, pens or pencils, clay or play-dough, other props and prizes if desired*

Leading through the Session

Straight Away

Explore the Bible passage.
Bibles; chalkboard or dry erase board, or butcher paper with large outline of body and markers

The Turn

Discuss getting back together.
Bibles

Leading beyond the Session

Home Stretch

Option 1 Discuss what you would do.
YOUNGER YOUTH   *Reproducible 2, pens or pencils*
Option 2 Brainstorm ways to remain steadfast in the faith.
OLDER YOUTH   *Chalkboard or dry erase board*

Finish Line

Option 1 Experience a time of reflection.
LITTLE PREP
Option 2 Play Spin and Tell.
MORE PREP   *Spinner from a game, poster board with covered questions that match the spinner*

SESSION 1

DOUBLE AGENT

Bible Passage
Colossians 1:15–23

Key Verses
[Jesus Christ] is the image of the invisible God, the firstborn over all creation. For by him all things were created … all things were created by him and for him.
—Colossians 1:15–16

Main Thought
God can be known through the person of Christ.

Bible Background

Although it may be difficult, it is important for us to imagine living in the first century after Christ and attempt to see what was going on in the life of the early church that prompted the writing of passages such as this text from Colossians. It has become conventional to refer to these verses as a *Christology*—that is, teaching about the nature or person of Christ. Because this instruction asserts in strong terms the relationship of Christ to God we call it a "high" Christology. Faithful reading of the Bible calls us to ask, "What would lead Paul to state this relationship so strongly?"

It is not inaccurate to refer to the first century church as "the Jesus movement." True enough, the gospel was being preached throughout Asia and in several European cities on the Mediterranean Sea. Tradition also says that the Apostle Thomas carried the gospel to the East as far as India. However, we should not let the gospel's rapid spread create the impression that either Christianity or the church were fully formed by the conclusion of the first century. Many questions and problems persisted. Some of these issues were matters of organization, and we find letters such as 1 and 2 Timothy dealing with those. Other issues concerned emerging Christian practices. Paul's letter to the Galatian Christians dealt with the vexing problem of the status of Gentiles in the new Christian community: Were Gentile converts expected to follow the rituals and practices of Judaism? Other practices also had to be established. For example, questions arose among early Christians concerning the practice of baptism. While immersion was preferred, what were believers to do when a large enough body of water was not available? Did it make a difference whether the water was "living" (i.e., running) or a quiet pool? Was the water for baptism to be cool or warm? Some of these questions may seem inconsequential to a contemporary believer, but they illustrate the fact that almost everything about the new Jesus movement had to be defined and established. This challenge was true not only concerning organization and practices but also in the realm of teaching about the nature of Christ.

Paul, Peter, and other leaders whose names are familiar to us from the pages of the New Testament were not the only people spreading the gospel of Jesus Christ. It is important to remember that the gospel spread first on the basis of oral tradition and reasoning from the Greek translation of the Old Testament, the Septuagint. It is during this period that Paul wrote his letters. Following this the Gospels were written, but several interpretations of Jesus' life and ministry appeared in addition to the four canonical gospels of Mark, Luke, Matthew, and John (listed here in their probable sequence of writing). Of those non-canonical gospels some offered highly irregular or heterodox interpretations of the Christ. Among those there circulated the notion that the Christ had not actually become incarnate but had only appeared in the likeness of the human Jesus. Another interpretation assumed that because the highest of the gods could not be contaminated with human flesh, it was a lesser divinity that had become incarnate in Jesus of Nazareth. In the first century, with so much about the Jesus movement yet to be determined, these rival interpretations could claim to be just as legitimate as the gospel proclaimed by Peter, Paul, and others. Texts such as this from Colossians were written to counter such interpretations and lay the foundation of orthodox Christian belief about the nature of the Redeemer. They affirm a real incarnation of God himself, such that Martin Luther could say of Jesus Christ, "You should look into this man's face and say, 'This is God.' "

OPTION 1 (LITTLE PREP)

Consider the roles we fulfill.

Ask each student to find a partner. Encourage the students to interview one another in their pairs, each person preparing to introduce the other to the rest of the class. Ask the students to focus on descriptions, not biographical information, and to find as many ways as possible to describe one another. For example: "Rosa is a daughter and a sister. She is a painter. She is a student at Cloverdale High School. She is a leader of a girl's Bible study." After compiling information about their partners, invite students to briefly describe one another to the rest of the class.

Point out that your students found many different ways to describe one another. Ask, **Is John the painter any different from John the mechanic (use examples from your class)? Why or why not?**

Say, **The same person often fulfills different roles in life.**

Warm Up

· ·

OPTION 2 (MORE PREP)

Discuss different representations.

Show your students a picture of a car and ask them to describe what they see. Next, show a video clip of a car and ask students to describe what they see. Now, show a model of a car and ask students to describe what they see. Finally, take your students outside and show them an actual car. Ask them to describe what they see. (***Note:*** This illustration will work especially well if you can use the same make, model, and color of car for each part.)

Say, **We just saw several different representations of a car. Were they all the same thing? Why or why not?** Point out that the picture, the video, and the model are all true representations of the real thing. They each really represent a car, but the car outside is the car in its real, tangible form—something that can be touched and driven.

Say, **In life we sometimes use different forms or images to represent a certain thing.**

Note:

There is a color picture and video of a car on the Digital BRIDGES CD.

Starting Line

Website:

See http://
en.wikipedia.
org/wiki/Con-
servation_of_
mass.

OPTION 1 (YOUNGER YOUTH)

Look at different forms.

Display for your students a cup of water, some pieces of ice, and a container of steaming water. Ask students if all three of these items are the same. After class members have responded, point out that water, ice, and steam are all made of the compound H_2O. According to the law of conservation of mass, mass cannot be created or destroyed, but can change its form. The heat causing water to turn into steam or the cold causing water to form ice changes only the *form* of the matter. The water, ice, and steam are still made up of the same substance, even though they do not look the same or have all the same properties.

Brainstorm with your students about other things that can be present in different forms. Examples include *carbon* (coal or diamonds), *clay* or *playdough*, and *bread* (which can be made into toast). After recording students' responses on the board, say, **Today we are going to consider this concept as we look at the person of Christ.**

OPTION 2 (OLDER YOUTH)

Perform some proverbs.

Prior to class, copy "Proverbs" (Reproducible 1) and cut the sheet apart as instructed. Divide the class into teams of two or three students each. Give each team a proverb and challenge the teams to spend a few minutes thinking about how to present their proverbs in as many different forms as possible without losing the original message. For example, a particular proverb could be expressed by speaking it, writing it, acting it out, and singing it. You can furnish paper and pens or pencils, clay or playdough, or other props for students to use. Invite groups to present their proverbs to the rest of the class. If time allows, give each group additional proverbs to work with. If you wish, you can award candy or other small prizes to the group that presents the most forms while maintaining the original message.

Brainstorm with your students about some individual things that can be present in different forms. Examples include *carbon* (coal or diamonds), *clay* or *playdough*, and *bread* (which can be made into toast). After recording students' responses on the board, say, **Today we are going to consider this concept as we look at the person of Christ.**

Explore the Bible passage.

Ask a student to read aloud Colossians 1:15–20. If possible, post on the wall a sheet of butcher paper with a large outline in the shape of a human body. Invite some other students to write within the outline the descriptions of Christ that they hear in the Bible passage (*image of the invisible God, firstborn over all creation, creator of everything, before all things, holding all things together, head of the church, the beginning, supreme in everything, containing the fullness of God, reconciling all things to himself,* and *making peace through his shed blood*). If you do not have the butcher paper outline, you can write the descriptions on a chalkboard or dry erase board. Invite students to share which of these images they find most important, most powerful, or easiest to understand.

Straight Away

Say, **This passage in Colossians gives us many descriptions of Christ. If you could generalize these characteristics, summarizing them in one word, what would you say?** Answers will vary. These descriptions are all positive and center around the power of Christ, the presence of Christ, and the relationship of Christ to God and to us.

Now invite a student to read Colossians 1:15 again. Ask, **What do you think this means? How can someone be an image of something that's invisible?** Christ is not a physical reflection of God ("God is spirit"—see John 4:24), but Christ is the perfect and full reflection of the eternal, all-powerful, all-present, reconciling God of love and peace.

Now ask a student to read aloud Colossians 1:21–23. Discuss the following questions:

- **According to this passage, what was our status before Christ came?** We were alienated from God. We were God's enemies.
- **Why did we have that status?** We were alienated because of our evil behavior (verse 21). Help your students to understand the concept of alienation (being from or relating to another person or place, a stranger, being incompatible with someone or with your surroundings). "Aliens" from another planet or aliens from another country illustrate this idea. Help your students to also understand that each of us is guilty of "evil behavior" or sin (Romans 3:23); even one bad thought a day tallies up to hundreds of sins in a year. The wages of our sin is death, but God offers life, through Christ, to those who will accept the gift (Romans 6:23).
- **What has God done for us through his supreme and awesome Son, Jesus Christ?** God has reconciled us to himself and made us holy and spotless in his sight, free from accusation because of our sin. The death of the sinless Christ has paid the price for our own sin, and the blood of Christ covers our sin in God's sight.
- **There is a very important "if" in this passage, and it relates to us. Where is it, and what does it mean?** See verse 23. Christ has made the sacrifice, but it does us good only if we "continue in [our] faith, established and firm, not moved from the hope held out in the gospel." Ask your students to imagine standing before God at the end of their lives and being able to say, "I made it! There were some troubles along the way, but I held on to my faith!" Eternal life is a gift that is worth keeping at all costs.

• **Why would Paul become a "servant" to this gospel, giving his whole life to preach it?** Christ entered Paul's life in a dramatic way (see Acts 9:1–31). Paul knew personally the power of Christ to heal and to save. God's calling was first in Paul's life, directing his thoughts, his words, and his actions.

Say, **Paul knew that in Christ we have the chance to be in relationship with our Creator, the God of the universe.**

The Turn

Discuss getting back together.

Write the word *reconcile* on the board and ask students to define the word according to their own understanding. Emphasize that to be reconciled is to be restored to friendship or harmony—to "get back together." Invite students to share any experiences they have had with reconciliation. Now write *requirements of reconciliation* on the board and ask students for ideas about what needs to happen in order for reconciliation to occur. Responses might include *forgiveness, a humble heart, a change of attitude or behavior,* and so forth. Remind students that this was the purpose of Christ having a physical form. Because of the sacrifice he made, we can be brought into a relationship with God. Ask students to recall our condition before Christ (alienated, evil, and enemies of the Lord.)

Invite a student to read aloud Romans 5:8. Ask, **What was the motivation behind Christ dying to reconcile us to God?** Christ died for us—while we were still in sin and selfishness—because of God's great love for us. Now invite a student to read aloud Romans 5:9–11. Ask, **What was Paul saying here? If God reconciled us to himself while we were still God's enemies, what else do we need?** Paul was saying, "You've had only a small taste of the goodness of God. God loved you so much that Christ died for you while you were still God's enemy. Now that you are walking with God, his power and presence in your life will be incredible!"

Say, **God was loving you and working in your life before you even knew him.**

Leading beyond the Session

Home Stretch

OPTION 1 (YOUNGER YOUTH)
Discuss what you would do.

Distribute copies of "What Would You Do?" (Reproducible 2) and invite students to work in small groups to analyze each situation. If time is limited, you can assign a different situation to each group. After a few minutes, bring the groups back together and ask, **What are some practical things that each of us can do to remain steadfast and firm in our faith?** Remaining solid in anything requires commitment—time and effort. God has provided the guidance of the Bible, the dialogue of prayer, the fellowship of the church, and the presence of the Holy Spirit to strengthen our faith. Knowing what we are committed to before we get into a situation and communicating frequently and honestly with those who share our faith commitments can help to keep us strong.

Say, **God gave his very best for us—and he asks for our very best.**

12

Option 2 (Older Youth)

Brainstorm ways to remain steadfast in the faith.

Ask your students to brainstorm together ways to remain steadfast in their faith. Write the responses on the board as they are given. Point out that remaining solid in anything requires commitment—time and effort. God has provided the guidance of the Bible, the dialogue of prayer, the fellowship of the church, and the presence of the Holy Spirit to strengthen our faith. Knowing what we are committed to before we get into a situation and communicating frequently and honestly with those who share our faith commitments can help to keep us strong.

After a good list has been compiled, invite students to pick the top five ways and to summarize them in a short phrase. If time allows, students could write and perform a short skit emphasizing the five ways.

Say, **God gave his very best for us—and he asks for our very best.**

Option 1 (Little Prep)

Experience a time of reflection.

Ask your students if they have ever looked in a funhouse mirror that distorts and stretches a reflection or if they have ever tried to look in a bathroom mirror that is all fogged up. Point out that the image reflected by a mirror is only true if the mirror is true and unobstructed. Jesus Christ reflects to us perfectly the image of God. We, in turn, should reflect that image to our family, friends, and the rest of the world.

Finish Line

Close the session with a time of reflection. Ask students to think about the opportunity they have to journey with Jesus Christ, the perfect reflection of God. What is keeping them from receiving God's love and reflecting it to others? Are there some things obstructing the view? The closer we walk to Christ, the more fully we will know and experience God's love and power in our lives, until it overflows wherever we go.

Lead your students in a time of prayer, asking that God would transform these youth as they understand and embrace God's sacrifice for them. Pray also that the lives of your students would be a daily testimony of God's transforming power to the people around them.

Note:

Don't forget to distribute copies of the Portable Sanctuary to students before they go.

OPTION 2 (MORE PREP)

Play Spin and Tell.

Bring to class a spinner from a game such as Twister. Post on the wall a poster board with questions relating to today's discussion. Following are some suggestions:

- *What gives you joy in your life?*
- *How would you describe Jesus to someone who doesn't know who he is?*
- *How do you feel about Christ's sacrifice for you?*
- *What does the phrase "standing firm" mean to you?*
- *What spoke to you the most from our discussion today?*
- *Is there any way that you think you should live differently?*

Cover the different questions with paper corresponding to the colors, numbers, or other designations on your spinner. Tape these covers over the questions so that they can be removed and then reattached. Invite students to take turns spinning the spinner, uncovering the corresponding questions, and then answering those questions. You may wish to offer students the option of saying "pass" if they do not wish to respond. Each participant should cover the question back up before the next person takes a spin.

After everyone has had a chance to spin and answer, conclude the session by encouraging students to participate in a time of prayer for one another, focusing on the needs or responses that were shared. Close the prayer time by asking God to transform these youth as they understand and embrace God's sacrifice for them. Pray also that the lives of your students would be a daily testimony of God's transforming power to the people around them.

> *Note:*
>
> Don't forget to distribute copies of the Portable Sanctuary to students before they go.

Proverbs

The early bird gets the worm.

An apple a day keeps the doctor away.

All work and no play makes Jack a dull boy.

A stitch in time saves nine.

Don't count your chickens before they are hatched.

Every dog has his day.

Finders, keepers; losers, weepers.

The bigger they are, the harder they fall.

Laughter is the best medicine.

A bird in the hand is worth two in the bush.

Beggars can't be choosers.

Birds of a feather flock together.

Curiosity killed the cat.

Don't put all your eggs in one basket.

Every picture tells a story.

First come, first served.

What Would You Do?

Situation 1

Cassie had waited so long for a friend. She couldn't believe it when Melanie started hanging out with her. Melanie is one of the most popular girls at school! Cassie has been a big help to Melanie with her school-work, and Melanie has helped Cassie with fashion suggestions, makeup tips, and new friends. People notice Cassie at school now—even some of the guys, and they never have before. One night before exams Mel stayed out late partying. She called Cassie before class on her cell. "Cassie, you gotta help me pass this test today!" Melanie said. "If you don't, my parents are gonna know I was out late last night and they'll kill me! I know I can trust you to help me out."

If you were Cassie, what would you do?

Situation 2

Xhou Xi Min is a pastor in China, where it is illegal to do any ministry that is not approved by the government. He was arrested last month for leading a Bible study. While he was in prison, news reached him that his eleven-year-old son had been struck with a serious illness. The family has no income because of Pastor Min's incarceration, so the child may die. Pastor Min feels that he can endure the torture and the poor conditions in prison, but his heart is heavy knowing his child is suffering and that he may never see him again. He also knows that there is a chance his child could recover if he could just receive help. The government has promised to release Pastor Min if he signs a confession denouncing his faith and promising not to practice religion.

If you were Pastor Min, what would you do?

Situation 3

Tio's parents have encouraged him not even to date non-Christians. "Son," his dad said, "once you're in a relationship it becomes a lot more difficult to set boundaries and follow your faith. It's better to make a decision like this before you even begin to date." Tio agreed and he has gone out with Christian girls only. The annual Sadie's dance is coming up in a month, a dance where the guys are asked by the girls. If Missy Parker (a girl Tio knows from church) asked him to go, he'd say "yes" in a heartbeat, but Missy has to be out of town that weekend. Unexpectedly, Vanessa Pinkston has asked Tio to go. Vanessa is gorgeous, but Tio knows she is not a believer. When Tio told his friend Jermaine the reason for his hesitation, Jermaine said, "Are you crazy? Vanessa is hot! What's wrong with you?! It's just one dance—no big deal."

If you were Tio, what would you do?

Portable Sanctuary

Day 1

Caught in the Act

Caught! Her heart stuck in her throat and she could barely breathe. Before she could even gather her garments around her, they grabbed her, pulling her by her hair, her cloak, her arms. As she was being dragged through the door, it all swirled around her— *"What's going to happen to me?"* Suddenly shoved into the dirt, she gulped hot tears as she prayed for her life. Someone pulled at her: "Stand up, trash!" as calls for her death rang out. Then suddenly there was silence. A man was writing in the dirt. *"What's going to happen to me?"* her heart again cried. The man spoke briefly and the crowd began to filter away. The love she had searched for in the arms of many men was found here—in the dirt. Would she ever be the same again?

Questions and Suggestions

- Read John 8:1–11. When you read this account, what glimpse of God do you get from the words, attitudes, and actions of God's image—Christ?

- Have you ever experienced being the one in the middle of others' accusations? Have you ever been the one holding the stones? Pray that your treatment of others will reflect the generous forgiveness of God.

Day 2

Blemishes

The Book of Leviticus provides many insights into the holiness of God. For example, a priest—the one responsible to offer sacrifices to God on behalf of the people—had to remain clean and undefiled. No child from the line of Aaron who had any kind of physical defect was to serve

---

- What was the last time you felt very discouraged? What brought you to that place? Even if that time is now, write a prayer of thanksgiving to God for giving his very best for you.

N O T E S

as priest. In fact, such a person could not even come close to the altar. The offerings of the people were also to be without defect. If this was not observed, then the offering was deemed unacceptable. Colossians 1 says that because of Christ's sacrifice, we are presented without blemish to God. We can approach God because God has made the way for us to be holy.

Questions and Suggestions

• Read Leviticus 21:21–23 and Leviticus 22:17–20. Does this seem like a harsh or unfair policy? Why would God care so much about the physical condition of the priests or the sacrifices?

• Think for a moment about the blemishes in your own life. Thank God for providing a way for you to enter God's presence, pure and holy in God's sight.

Day 3
Standing Firm

On October 29, 2005, Ida Yarni Sambue, 15; Theresia Morangki, 16; and Alfrita Poliwo, 19, were on their way to Poso Christian High School in Sulawesi, Indonesia. That morning they were attacked and decapitated, without provocation. They were not out preaching on the streets or converting Muslims behind closed doors. Their only "crime" was that they were not Muslim. They were just teens—going to school. However, because they were not Muslim and attended a Christian school, they lost their lives. *Do most of us really know what it means to stand firm for our faith?*

Questions and Suggestions

• Read Matthew 10:22. According to this verse, why are Christians hated? Who will be saved?

• How could the families and friends of these girls from Indonesia stand firm? Say a prayer for the families of these girls and for other persecuted Christians who are being challenged daily to stand firm in their faith.

Day 4
Reliability

If you are reading this Portable Sanctuary right now then you are relying on your eyes to pass the words along to your brain. You are also relying on light from some source to illuminate the words on the page. To do even this simple task you were dependent on something. Human beings rely on oxygen, food, and water to sustain life, and we rely on many other things such as transportation, energy, and relationships in our daily lives. When something is not there that we usually rely on, what happens? Sometimes we get annoyed and frustrated; sometimes there is chaos, sometimes even death. But in the end, God is all we need to rely on.

Questions and Suggestions

• Read Philippians 4:19. What kinds of riches are ours in Christ Jesus?

• Today, keep a list of all the things that you rely on. At the end of the day, review the list and circle any things that you think you rely on too much. Is there anything or anyone that you should rely on more?

Day 5
Best thing?

"Nothing good *ever* happens to me!" Sometimes the journey of life brings pain and discouragement. Every person on earth has experienced loss, disappointment, grief, and hardships. But, as creations of God, we have the greatest reason for joy—even as life brings its challenges. Because of Christ's sacrifice, we have a reason to rejoice. The life that is Christ's can be our life too. Circumstances come and go, but the joy that comes from walking with God can last forever.

Questions and Suggestions

• Read a portion of Peter's sermon found in Acts 2:22–28. In Peter's words, how was Jesus Christ the best thing that had ever happened? What difference does this make for our lives?

Leading into the Session

Warm Up

Option 1
LITTLE PREP
Let the oldest always win.
One main prize and some smaller prizes for the rest of class (optional)

Option 2
MORE PREP
Create imprints.
Leaves, various patterned objects with texture, white paper, crayons, scissors, tape

Starting Line

Option 1
YOUNGER YOUTH
Picture a firstborn.
Chalkboard or dry erase board, pictures of famous "firstborns"

Option 2
OLDER YOUTH
Look at a reflection.
Large mirror, two chairs, sheet or other barrier, a volunteer not well-known to the class

Leading through the Session

Straight Away

Explore the Bible passage.
Bibles

The Turn

Discuss: Who do you say Christ is?
Bibles, Reproducible 1, pens or pencils

Leading beyond the Session

Home Stretch

Option 1
YOUNGER YOUTH
Piece it all together.
Heavy cardstock paper, scissors, markers, zip-lock plastic bags

Option 2
OLDER YOUTH
Discuss how we should live.
Reproducible 2, pens or pencils; Bible, background music (optional)

Finish Line

Option 1
LITTLE PREP
Participate in a role play.
Reproducible 1

Option 2
MORE PREP
Engage in a religious discussion.
Special guests of other faiths

SESSION 2

JESUS: THE REFLECTION OF GOD

Bible Passage
Hebrews 1:1–9

Key Verse
In these last days [God] has spoken to us by his Son, whom he appointed heir of all things, and through whom he made the universe.
—Hebrews 1:2

Main Thought
Jesus Christ gives us a glimpse of the glory of God.

Bible Background

The Book called "Hebrews" is unique among the books of the New Testament, the rest of which each take the form of either a gospel or a letter. Hebrews is neither, but is instead a sermon or discourse demonstrating the unsurpassable nature of Christ and his sacrifice on the cross. Hebrews characteristically alternates theological or doctrinal points such as this with exhortations concerning the quality of the life of discipleship that necessarily follows from such theological instruction. Thus Christ's absolutely unique and unrepeatable sacrifice calls his followers to lives of mature, faithful discipleship. One historical note before considering this text: Hebrews was something of a controversial addition to the canonical books of the New Testament. The fact that it is an anonymous treatise was a liability in the eyes of ancient Christians. Nevertheless, the book was included in lists of authoritative books that were published in the fourth century and which conventionally are employed as evidence of a New Testament book's canonical status.

Hebrews 1:1–9 is an exalted statement about the relationship of Christ to God. In these opening verses of the discourse, interestingly, Christ is not identified by name. It is not until 2:9 that we will read the name Jesus. "Until then we read of the One whom Hebrews refers to as "the Son." As much as this might seem a matter of fact to Christians reading this text from a distance of two thousand years, it was no simple assertion. Hebrews' theme of the unsurpassable nature of Christ's ministry begins with the words "he has spoken to us by his Son." God had previously spoken on many occasions and through various means—often through his prophets. The incarnation of the Word of God in Jesus of Nazareth dramatically altered the manner of God's speech and with that God's revelation—his self-disclosure—to human beings. Prophets and apostles are ambassadors in that they speak a word that has been given to them by another. The Son is the revelatory Word himself.

He is the Word by and through whom God called the universe into being. Not content to compare the Word of the Son to the words of prophets, Hebrews proceeds to describe the nature of the relationship between the Son and God. Not unlike the way in which the sun's rays are its extended energy, so the Son radiates God's glory and exactly represents the very being of God.

There may have been those who interpreted Jesus as an angel or some other created heavenly being. To counter such teaching Hebrews makes an extended comparison through the use of rhetorical questions and passages from the Old Testament (remember, first-century Christians read and interpreted the Old Testament as their Bible) to point out that the Son is much more than an angel. Hebrews draws from the Psalms, Samuel, and Deuteronomy to anchor the conclusion that the Son is God himself.

Christians annually celebrate Advent to mark the beginning of a new year. What better way to begin the year than by celebrating the birth of our Savior? That we celebrate the birth of Christ annually risks the possibility that we will lose sight of its miraculous nature. God, not an angel, became a human being—not an illusion but flesh and blood. This is a great mystery, so much so that the thirteenth-century theologian Thomas Aquinas considered it and the doctrine of the Trinity to be the two matters of Christian doctrine that reason could neither explain nor comprehend. Hebrews teaches that none other than the Son of God has come among us to save and reveal. That is a wondrous miracle indeed.

OPTION 1 (LITTLE PREP)

Let the oldest always win.

Warm Up

Prior to class, determine which of your regular students is the oldest. (*Note:* If you have any new students and feel that one of them may be oldest, ask them to write down their personal information—including birth date—for your records.) When class begins, announce that there are going to be some competitions and the winner of the greatest number of competitions will receive a prize. Hold two or three competitions that will work in the space you have and with the number of students you have. When explaining a contest, do not tell the students how it is won. Just say that the point is to reach the goal. Possible ideas include, but are not limited to:

- Race—a timed race from one point to another (variations could include racing by hopping on one foot, racing using the crab crawl, and so forth).
- Shoe pile-up—students put all their shoes in a pile across the room and then race to find their own shoes and put them back on.
- Balloon challenge—students blow up balloons and tie them to their ankles. At your word, the students try to pop each other's balloons while keeping their own intact.
- Whistling contest—students fill their lungs with air and see who can whistle the longest on one breath. No one may pause or take an additional breath of air.
- Buzz—students sit in a circle and begin to count, one number per person, going around the circle. When the number seven or any multiple of seven is up, the person counting must say "Buzz" and not the number. (For example: one, two, three, four, five, six, buzz, eight, nine, ten, eleven, twelve, thirteen, buzz, and so forth.) Students should count as rapidly as possible; anyone who makes a mistake is eliminated and the counting begins again from one.

After each competition, announce the oldest student as the winner even if that person did not come in first. Refuse to explain yourself until all the competitions are completed. If you wish, give a big prize to the "firstborn" and smaller prizes to the rest of the class.

Afterwards, discuss the experience with your students. Ask, **Why do you think _____ won all of the contests? Do you think this was fair?** Explain that throughout history, the firstborn son has traditionally been the individual who inherited the estate, even when it might have seemed unfair. In Bible times, the firstborn received a double portion of the assets of the father. He also received the responsibility of caring for that property and for the other family members.

Say, **Being the firstborn can be a position of great honor.**

OPTION 2 (MORE PREP)

Create imprints.

Provide white paper and crayons and invite students to make imprints of leaves or other objects by rubbing with a crayon on white paper placed over the objects. Encourage class members to be creative and to look around the room or outdoors to determine if there is anything else they can copy. Ask students to cut their creations out and to tape them up in a designated area. As you all observe what has been created by the class, ask, **How are these imprints the same as the objects they were made from? How are they different?**

Point out that although the paper is much different than the object itself, there is a representation of the object on the paper. One can get a sense of the actual object by looking at the imprint.

Say, **These imprints can let others know what objects we have been dealing with.**

Starting Line

OPTION 1 (YOUNGER YOUTH)

Picture a firstborn.

Bring to class some pictures of famous firstborns and post them or pass them around. (A Google search can provide the images you need.) Draw students' attention to the photos and ask the class what these people have in common. Write the letters *F-I-R-S-T-B-O-R-N* vertically on the board and explain that all the photos show firstborn children. Ask students to think about the firstborns whom they know personally (perhaps some of them are firstborn children) and to consider common characteristics or stereotypes of firstborns by using the letters of the word *firstborn*. As answers are offered, write them on the board. Some possibilities:

> *First*
> *Interesting*
> *Rich*
> *Spoiled*
> *Talented*
> *Blessed*
> *Oldest*
> *Rewarded*
> *Normal*

Next, ask students to think about Christ specifically. Are there any of the listed firstborn characteristics that are demonstrated in Christ?

Say, **Let's consider the position of Christ as the firstborn of God.**

OPTION 2 (OLDER YOUTH)

Look at a reflection.

Set up a large mirror in the front of your group. Ask a volunteer to come forward. Place this person in a chair where he or she can see the mirror and anything reflected in it. Ask the volunteer to close his or her eyes. Now, bring in someone who is not a member of the class and is preferably not familiar to your students. This person should sit silently in a chair so that his or her reflection is visible to your volunteer, while you use a sheet or other barrier to block direct sight. The idea is to allow the student to see only the reflection in the mirror. Ask the student to open his or her eyes and to describe the person in the mirror in as detailed a manner as possible. Now, remove the barrier so that the real person can be seen.

Discuss the following questions:

To the student volunteer
- **Would you describe this person the same way now that you see him or her in person?**
- **Are there any things that you missed by not seeing him or her in person?**

To everyone
- **How accurate (or close to life) is a reflection?**
- **What are the differences between a reflection and the real thing?** Explain that a reflection is a glimpse of the real thing. It is an accurate depiction in some ways but is limited or different in others.

Say, **Let's see how Jesus Christ is the exact representation of God.**

Leading through the Session

Explore the Bible passage.

Read together Hebrews 1:1–9. If you wish, you can have one student read the narrative portions and another read the Old Testament verses that are quoted. Discuss the following questions:

Straight Away

- **How did God initially speak to his people?** "Through the prophets at many times and in various ways" (verse 1). Ask if any students can name some of the Old Testament prophets who spoke for God. Examples include Moses, Isaiah, Elijah, Elisha, Isaiah, Jeremiah, and all of the individuals for whom the Old Testament books from Ezekiel on are named.
- **What kinds of things did the prophets speak about?** Prophets often rebuked the people for their unfaithfulness to God, but they also gave instruction on God's will for the people, brought words of encouragement and hope from God, and sometimes foretold specifically what God would do in the future.
- **What is the "new way" that God has spoken to us now, and how is it better?** God has spoken to us by his Son, Jesus Christ. Jesus is the "radiance of God's glory and the exact representation of [God's] being, sustaining all

things" (verse 3). He is superior not only to the prophets of old but even to the angels who minister in the very presence of God. Because of this, and because Jesus now sits "at the right hand of the Majesty in heaven" (i.e., in God's very presence), there is no limitation with him and no room for error or misinterpretation between him and God. This does not mean, of course, that human beings never misinterpret what Jesus says or does!

- **What does it mean to be the "radiance" of something? What does Jesus radiate?** To radiate is to shine, to send out light or heat from a source. Jesus radiates God's glory—in other words, he shows us the character, the image, and the person of God.

- **What does it mean to sustain something, and what kind of sustaining does Jesus Christ do?** To sustain is to support or nourish something, to hold it up and keep it going. The Son sustains *all things*. Our lives, the function of the universe, and the laws of gravity, thermodynamics, physics, and chemistry are all kept in place and kept going by the powerful word of God. And many people will testify to the fact that God has sustained them *personally* during times of heartache and tragedy. When we can count on nothing else in this world, we can count on God to be there for us.

- **Why do you think the author of Hebrews found it necessary to prove that Jesus is different from (and superior to) the angels?** Prior to Jesus there had never been (and there never has been since) anything like him— God himself, made flesh and walking on the earth. As people struggled to explain just who and what Jesus was and how he related to God, it is possible that some people identified Jesus as some sort of angel. Hebrews shows us that this was not the case.

- **How did the author of Hebrews substantiate the claim that Christ is higher than the angels?** Anyone can have an opinion—but the writer of Hebrews used the Word of God to demonstrate that Christ is indeed above the angels. Ask students to describe how these Old Testament passages support this claim. Explain that to a Jew or a Christian in the first century, the authority of the Bible (at that time just the Old Testament) was undisputed.

- **How would you summarize the qualities that are attributed to Jesus Christ in this passage?** Jesus Christ is the Son of God, the radiance of God, the exact representation of God, the sustainer of all things, superior to the angels, reigning forever. The author of Hebrews used the most positive of terms to describe Christ.

Say, **In Christ we can see the glory and majesty of God.**

Discuss: *Who do you say Christ is?*

Invite a student to read aloud Matthew 16:13–16. Ask, **How did people see Christ during the time he was on earth?** Some thought he was John the Baptist, Elijah, Jeremiah, or some other prophet; Peter proclaimed that Jesus was the Son of God.

Divide students into four groups and give each group a copy of "What Do They Believe?" (Reproducible 1). Assign each group a different religion and give them time to review the appropriate information. After a few minutes, allow the groups to share their findings with the rest of the class. Ask students what similarities they see in these religious beliefs and how Christianity stands out from the rest. Emphasize that in no other faith is it believed that God came to earth as a man to redeem us.

Ask another student to read John 8:12–18. Explain that the Pharisees challenged Jesus' claim to be the Son of God by saying that Christ could not be his own witness. Discuss the following questions:

- **Based on what we have studied today in Hebrews, would you say that Christ's testimony about his identity is valid? Explain.**
- **Why do you think it was (and still is) difficult for some people to accept Jesus' identity?**
- **Besides his words, in what other ways did Christ establish his identity?** Jesus fulfilled prophecy, healed the sick, cast out demons, cared for the outcasts, raised the dead, and was himself raised from the dead—yet because of jealousy, ignorance, or the things that Jesus taught, some people chose not to believe. Many people today refuse to believe in Jesus without physically seeing him, and some still reject Jesus because of the things his teaching asks of us.

Say, **Each of us must decide who Christ is and what he means to us.**

The Turn

Note:

This reproducible will be used again if using FINISH LINE, Option 1.

Leading beyond the Session

OPTION 1 (YOUNGER YOUTH)

Piece it all together.

Ask the class to divide into groups of three or four students each. Invite each group to design a puzzle on cardstock paper. Each puzzle should provide clues to the identity of Christ and should be as creative as possible. Groups should cut their puzzles apart and put the pieces of each puzzle in a zip-lock plastic bag. The bags can be decorated festively if you are teaching this session at Christmastime.

As students are working, discuss the following questions:

- **What "clues" are present in the Scriptures to direct readers to the identity of Christ?** Christ's fulfillment of prophecy, his own words and teachings, his miracles and healings, his resurrection, and the testimony of the New Testament authors.
- **How should we live when we have discovered the identity of Christ (in other words, when we have "put the puzzle together")?** If we have

Home Stretch

Note:

If possible, you can provide an opportunity for groups to share their puzzles with a younger class.

discovered and believed in who Christ really is, then we should live in obedience to his teachings.

Say, **Through Jesus Christ, the reflection of God's glory can shine in our own lives.**

. . . .

OPTION 2 (OLDER YOUTH)
Discuss how we should live.

Distribute to students copies of "How Then Should We Live?" (Reproducible 2), or show it as a projection. Ask class members to take some time to consider how the identity of Christ should impact our lives. **Do we just need to make an intellectual decision to follow him, or is there something more? Is it a change of heart? a change of attitude? Some people have sold all their possessions in order to fully follow Christ—is that necessary for each of us?** Give your students a few minutes to think about who Christ is and how that knowledge should impact their lives. You may wish to play some contemplative music softly in the background.

After students have had time to respond, ask if any of them would like to share their thoughts. Allow a few moments for personal silent prayer. You can read aloud portions of Hebrews 1:1–9 during this time if you wish. When you are ready to move on, say, **Through Jesus Christ, the reflection of God's glory can shine in our own lives.**

Finish Line

OPTION 1 (LESS PREP)
Participate in a role play.

Explain that *apologetics* is the practice of knowing how to defend one's faith. It is very important to know what we believe and why. This enables us to answer concerns and questions that we face regularly in this world.

Ask for volunteers to participate in a role play. One student should be a Christian and another a person of one of the faiths found on Reproducible 1. The person of the other faith should question the Christian about the Christian's beliefs. If time permits, different students could complete short role plays involving each of the religions on the reproducible.

When you are finished, lead a discussion about how to best address the identity of Christ with others. Be sure your students know that a life lived in faithfulness to Christ—and a genuine love for and time investment in others—are strong factors in opening doors to share our faith. Close the session by leading your students in prayer for those who do not know Christ and by praying for the opportunity to share with others who Christ is.

Note:

Don't forget to distribute copies of the Portable Sanctuary to students before they go.

26

OPTION 2 (MORE PREP)

Engage in a religious discussion.

Your students may be unaware that people of other cultures and religions live around them and attend school with them. (This may even be true for those who attend private Christian schools.) Make arrangements for some visitors of other faiths to come to class; or, host another venue such as a "coffee shop evening" where students can gather with these visitors. This will give your class members the opportunity to learn from and share with people of other faiths. Share the following suggestions and information with your students before they interact with your guests:

- **We tend to stereotype members of other religions—and they often stereotype Christians! But *any* time we dialogue openly with another person, we have the chance to learn something—and to share something. This applies even when we talk with people of other faiths.**
- **Seek to find common emphases or teachings among Christianity and the other faiths represented.**
- **This is a good chance to understand better the teachings and practices of some other faiths. Ask the visitors how they came to be a part of their particular faith communities. What is it like in their worship services or other gatherings?**
- **We should be willing (and able) to share our faith at all times, even during this activity. However, the goal is to learn and share—not to preach or argue someone else into a conversion.**

You can use the following questions to debrief your students during your next meeting or right after your visitors have left:

- **What stood out to you about the people you spoke with?**
- **What did you learn that you never knew before?**
- **Did you share about your faith? How was it received?**
- **Why is it important for you to be sure about your faith and about who Christ is when you go "into the world"?**

Close the session by leading your students in prayer for those who do not know Christ and by praying for the opportunity to share with others who Christ is.

> *Note:*
>
> Don't forget to distribute copies of the Portable Sanctuary to students before they go.

The Church of God curriculum... BRIDGES!

The Church of God is a dynamic movement that promotes evangelism, holy living, and unity among all Christians worldwide. Warner Press publishes graded curriculum to help local congregations promote these values week after week.

Church of God pastors and teachers write BRIDGES to focus the truth of Scripture on current life issues. It's flexible enough to be used in traditional Sunday school, midweek study, or small groups. And BRIDGES offers teaching options for large congregations and small. Whether you have high-tech equipment or just a table and chairs, BRIDGES will work in your situation.

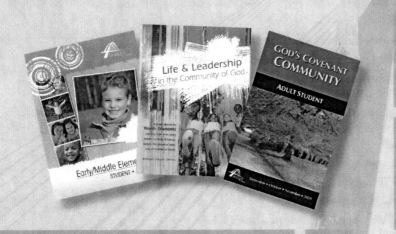

Different modules of BRIDGES are tailored to the needs of every grade level, from first grade through adult. Based on the Uniform Series of Scripture readings, its teaching plan takes you through every major theme of the Bible.

Here's a unique feature of BRIDGES: it teaches the history of the Church of God to all ages. From time to time, it brings all age groups together to hear stories of the movement, learn our songs, and discuss our most important values.

Order from... Warner Press

What Do They Believe?

Judaism

What they believe: Judaism teaches that the Old Testament is the word of God and that it prophesies the coming of a Messiah. However, the fulfillment of these Old Testament prophecies has not occurred—the Messiah has yet to come. Jews are to follow the Torah, or the first five books of Moses. They are to love God, obey the Law, and pray. Jewish people can trace their ancestry back through Abraham all the way to Adam and Eve. Historical Judaism is the ancestor and forerunner of the Christian faith. In current terminology, to call a person "Jewish" can mean that he or she is a physical descendent of the historical Jews—whether or not that person actually believes or practices the Jewish faith.
What they believe about Jesus: Most adherents of Judaism believe that Jesus did live on earth and was a religious man of great faith. However, he did not rise from the dead—and he was not the long-awaited Messiah.

Islam

What they believe: The holy book of the Islamic faith is the Qur'an, which includes the teachings of the prophet Mohammed. Islam teaches that Allah, the divine being, will determine who goes to paradise after death. There are five pillars of Islam, the things that a believer must do to gain favor with Allah. These include confessing that there is no other God but Allah and Mohammed is his prophet, praying five times a day, fasting for the month of Ramadan, giving alms to the poor, and making a pilgrimage (trip) to Mecca (in the Middle East). Muslims (people of Islamic faith) hold the Qur'an in highest regard, although they also consider the Jewish Scriptures (Old Testament) and the Injeel (New Testament) to be the word of Allah.
What they believe about Jesus: Jesus was born of a virgin and was a great prophet. However, his divinity is denied, as is the Crucifixion. Muslims believe there was an attempt on Jesus' life but he was delivered and raised up to heaven. Jesus is recognized as important but is considered to be below Mohammed. For Muslims, Jesus was just a great spiritual teacher.

Hinduism

What they believe: Hindus believe in *Brahman*—the unity of all things. Everything in the universe is part of a single divine entity, and all things are one with each other. Human beings are trapped in a cycle of birth, life, death, and rebirth. Through pure acts, thoughts, and devotion one can be reborn at a higher level. Eventually the devout can escape this cycle and achieve "enlightenment." *Karma* is the sum of one's good and bad deeds—and it determines how you will live your next life. Bad deeds might cause you to be reborn at a lower level—possibly as an animal. Suffering is
a natural consequence for bad deeds in past lives. Salvation can be achieved through knowledge, religious works, or devotion to a deity. There are many different deities—and therefore many different paths to salvation.
What they believe about Jesus: The teachings of Christ have been admired by many Hindus, including Mahatma Gandhi. Hindus can easily accept Jesus as divine, but there are *many* different deities and *many* acceptable paths to salvation. Hindus have difficulty accepting the concept of the Incarnation (God taking human form).

Buddhism

What they believe: Buddhism was founded on the teachings of the Buddha, Siddhārtha Gautama. Buddhists believe that there is no God or supreme being. All people are subject to suffering, which is caused by their desire for possessions and self-enjoyment. Buddhists seek to purify and train their minds by following the "Noble Eightfold Path," being released from their desires and therefore ending their suffering. Like Hindus, Buddhists believe that human beings are caught up in a cycle of birth-death-rebirth that is directed by karma. When we reach nirvana (enlightenment) then we are freed
from that cycle. Any person who has, without the help of others, become awakened to the principles of the Buddha's teachings is also called a buddha.
What they believe about Jesus: Since Buddhists do not believe in God, they do not believe in Christ as the Son of God. However, many Buddhists have been impressed by the teachings of Jesus and by the compassion demonstrated in his ministry. They are attracted by his example and his wisdom but only believe him to be a wise teacher—not divine.

How Then Should We Live?

How does the identity of Christ impact your life? How *should* it impact your life? Is it just a matter of making an intellectual decision to follow him, or is there something more? Is it a change of heart? a change of attitude? Some people have sold all their possessions in order to fully follow Christ—is that necessary for you? Take some time to think about it. Who is Christ to you? What should you do about it?

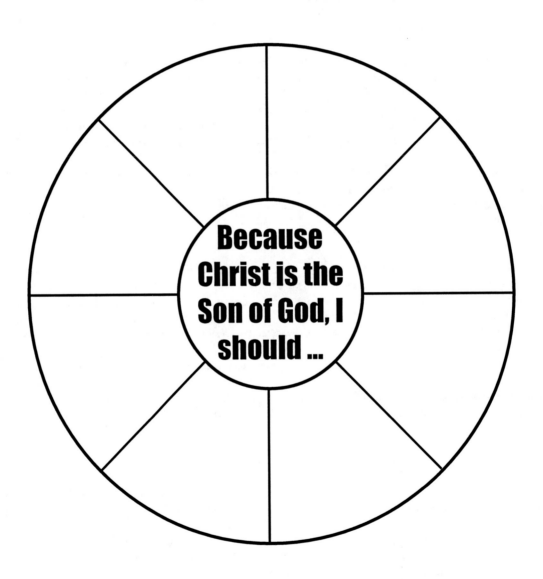

Because Christ is the Son of God, I should ...

Portable Sanctuary

Day 1

The Birthright

The sun was hot. Sweat ran down Esau's forehead, through his bushy red eyebrows, and into his eyes. After being in the field all day, he was tired and hungry. "I sure hope there's something to eat when I get home," he murmured. As he neared home he could see the tents—and smoke rising to the sky. That was a good sign! Esau rounded the corner to see his brother, Jacob, crouching over a pot of hot stew. "Jacob, give me some—quick! I'm dying of hunger!" Esau exclaimed.

Jacob thought for a minute, then said, "Give me your birthright, and I'll give you some stew." In the Israelite culture, the firstborn male child received the birthright—the best of the inheritance from his father. Being firstborn was really important.

"My birthright!" Esau hesitated for a second, but his hunger was too much. He traded away his future—and devoured the spicy stew.

Questions and Suggestions

- Read the account of this story in Genesis 25:29–34. What amazes you about this situation?
- Read Hebrews 1:1–9 again. What description of Christ's birthright do you find? What is his position?
- Thank God for the eternal inheritance that is shared with you through Christ.

Day 2

Seen or Unseen

In the Bible there are many accounts of angels. Often these angels came from God with specific messages about forthcoming miracles.

---

well-received by those who needed to hear it. But then God spoke to his people directly, through his Son. God may have thought, "Well, they wouldn't listen to my chosen prophets, but maybe they will listen to my own Son!" But even Christ was rejected—and he continues to be rejected. Oh, how God's heart must be breaking! Even today God continues to speak, through the Holy Spirit. Are you listening?

Questions and Suggestions

- Read what Christ says about "the Counselor"—the Holy Spirit—in John 16:5–16. How does the Holy Spirit give us an added glimpse of the heart of God? What role has the Holy Spirit played in your own life?
- Pray that God's Spirit will guide you into all truth and bring glory to God through your life.

N O T E S

Other times they came to serve and care for people in challenging circumstances. What did they look like? Sometimes they looked like you and me and were not even noticed. Other times they were so glorious and overwhelming that they could not even be looked at. Do they appear today? Television shows such as *Touched by an Angel* make it seem as if they are among us and look just like us. Contemporary novels describe them as mostly unseen, in constant battle against evil.

According to the Bible, angels are "ministering spirits sent to serve those who will inherit salvation" (Hebrews 1:14). Angels are below Christ. Only God and his Son are worthy of our worship and praise.

Questions and Suggestions

- When you think of the word *angel*, what pictures come to mind? Has anyone you know ever claimed to have had contact with an angel? What were the circumstances?
- Use a concordance to look through the Bible and find some stories and descriptions of angels. How have angels interacted with human beings? How have they served the Lord?
- Thank God for his care for you—through angels and in other ways.

Day 3
Joy to the World

Whenever Christmas begins to draw near, gifts are purchased and wrapped, the tree is trimmed, and carols are sung. But is Christmas just another holiday? What is the celebration really all about? Is it about Santa and Rudolph? As some people even seek to change the name of this very special day, it is good to consider: What is Christmas about? The celebration is about the King who came as a baby. He came as God in human form—an event that is pretty incomprehensible to human beings and impossible according to science! God gave up his throne, his status, and all that he had. He gave that up to come and be born in a stable and to eventually suffer an excruciatingly painful death on a cross. He did all that for you and me. Joy to the world!

Questions and Suggestions

- What are some ways that you usually celebrate Christmas? Do you have any special plans for next Christmas? What does this holiday mean to you?
- Write a prayer, thanking God for all he gave up for you.

Day 4
The Light of the World

Think about light for a moment. Is it important for you? What is light like? Light changes things. It radiates from its source, changing the darkened areas around it. Anything that is touched by light becomes clearer—it becomes seen and illuminated. Christ said that we are like light. We should not be ashamed of this light and try to hide it. The light that we have will give light to everyone. If we let God's light shine before others, they will see who God is. Because of how we live as we walk with Christ, others will get a glimpse of him through us. Hebrews 1:3 says that Jesus is "the radiance of God's glory and the exact representation of his being, sustaining all things by his powerful word." Because of Christ, we get a glimpse of the light of God—and we can see who God is. When Christ dwells in us, then we also reflect the light of God.

Questions and Suggestions

- Read Matthew 5:13–16. Are you shining brightly for Christ?
- Make a list of some ways that you can boldly show the light of Christ in your life.

Day 5
Are You Listening?

The writer of Hebrews points out that God initially spoke to his people through the prophets. These prophets took messages to the people and often these messages were not accepted. The prophets risked their lives in order to speak the truth of God—truth that was sometimes not

Leading into the Session

Warm Up

Option 1
LITTLE PREP
Compare the dark to the light.
Dark space that class members can visit, a flashlight or candle

Option 2
MORE PREP
Interact with a guest speaker.
Visitor who is blind

Starting Line

Option 1
YOUNGER YOUTH
Experience a challenge.
Two chairs, two buckets, several bags of cotton balls, a large serving spoon, blindfold

Option 2
OLDER YOUTH
Discover the properties of light.
Reproducible 1, pens or pencils, chalkboard or dry erase board; Digital BRIDGES CD, computer, and data projector (optional)

Leading through the Session

Straight Away

Explore the Bible passage.
Bibles, chalkboard or dry erase board

The Turn

Discuss light in the Bible.
Bibles

Leading beyond the Session

Home Stretch

Option 1
YOUNGER YOUTH
Talk about living in the light.

Option 2
OLDER YOUTH
Experience a candlelight service.
Bible, candles with drip guards, matches; Digital BRIDGES CD, computer, and data projector (optional)

Finish Line

Option 1
LITTLE PREP
Put the light on!
Reproducible 2

Option 2
MORE PREP
Create candles.
Clear wax, old saucepans, stovetop, crayons, knives, stirring sticks, candle molds, wicks, ribbon, hole punch, colored paper tags

---

SESSION 3

JESUS: THE LIGHT OF THE WORLD

Bible Passage
1 John 1:1 — 2:6

Key Verse
If we walk in the light, as he is in the light, we have fellowship with one another, and the blood of Jesus, his Son, purifies us from all sin.
—1 John 1:7

Main Thought
Jesus is the light, offering us new life in him.

Bible Background

The great ancient theologian Augustine wrote that 1 John "is very sweet to every healthy Christian heart that savors the bread of God, and it should constantly be in the mind of God's holy church.... The person who possesses the thing [love] which he hears about in this epistle must rejoice when he hears it. His reading will be like oil to a flame."[1] This letter is unique among the three Johanine letters because it carries no salutation, leading some ancient commentators to question whether John was its author. However, the similarities of 2 John and 3 John with the vocabulary, themes, and structure of 1 John indicate their common authorship along with the Gospel according to John.

Ancient Christian commentators interpreted the first five verses of 1 John in relation to the Christian doctrine of the Incarnation. The second-century theologian Clement interpreted the word *was* in 1:1, 2 as signifying eternity, "just as the Word himself, that is, the Son, which is one with the Father in equality of substance, is eternal and unmade."[2] In the time of Clement, many interpretations of Jesus' life and ministry were in circulation. Indeed, it was through the theological work of people such as Clement, his pupil Origen, and a host of others that the early church acquired the theological and philosophical vocabulary that enabled it to reach agreement on the doctrine of the Trinity in 325 at the Council of Nicea. It was very important to those who championed orthodox Christian teaching that the Word that became incarnate in Jesus be clearly understood as without a beginning. Thus Clement commented on 1:1, "For when he says 'that which was from the beginning' he is referring to the generation of the Son which has no beginning, because he exists co-eternally with the Father."[3] This may seem an extremely technical point of doctrine, but for early Christian teachers it was quite crucial. To the mind of Clement and others like him, if the Son was not divine in the same sense as the Father, then the Son could not raise us to eternal life in the Father.

It was just as critical that the ancient church understand that the incarnation of the Son was real rather than apparent. Augustine taught that the Son, the very life of God, became incarnate "so that what can be seen by the heart alone might be seen also by the eyes, in order that hearts might be healed."[4] The bishop-theologian Severus of Antioch wrote, "Given that this same John also said, 'No one has ever seen God,' how can he assure us that the living Word of life has been seen and touched? It is clear that it was in his incarnate and human form that he was visible and touchable. What was not true of him by nature became true of him in that way, for he is one and the same indivisible Word, both visible and invisible, and without diminishing in either respect he became touchable."[5] At Christmas we celebrate the mystery that the God whom no one has ever seen became touchable.

1. Quoted in *Ancient Christian Commentary on Scripture: New Testament, XI,* ed. by Gerald Bray (Downer's Grove, Ill: InterVarsity Press, 2000), 166.
2. Ibid.
3. Ibid.
4. Ibid., 167.
5. Ibid., 166.

OPTION 1 (LITTLE PREP)

Compare the dark to the light.

Take your students to a darkened room in the facility where you meet. A room without windows of any sort is preferable—the darker, the better. If the room is large enough, take all the students in at once and ask them to sit in a circle; if not, you can repeat the following instructions with a few students at a time.

Close the door and sit quietly in the darkness for a few moments. After a time of silence, ask students to speak out words that describe the darkness. This might include what the darkness feels like or looks like or any other impressions the students might have. After everyone has had a chance to share, light a candle or turn on a flashlight. (If you use a flashlight, direct the beam up toward the ceiling.) In silence, observe the light for a moment, then ask students to describe the light.

After you return to your classroom, say, **The introduction of light gives us a new perspective on our surroundings.**

Warm Up

· ·

OPTION 2 (MORE PREP)

Interact with a guest speaker.

Invite a person who is blind to visit the class. If possible, choose a person from your congregation or someone many of your students know. Ask your guest to share about himself or herself and about the experience of living with blindness. Following are some suggested questions to use:

- **Have you been blind for your entire life? What events or conditions led to your blindness?**
- **What doors of opportunity in your life have been closed because of your blindness? What doors have been opened?**
- **Honestly, how does our church (or your own church) do with making the church a welcoming, workable place for those without sight?**
- **What are some common misconceptions that other people have about people with blindness?**
- **Are you able to sense or perceive light at all? If so, how?**

Encourage your students to also ask their own questions of your guest. Be sure to point out that we are all affected by different sources of "light"—not just the sun or electric lights, but those things in our lives that make the way clear and help us see where to go. Even a person without eyesight has "guiding lights" in life—hearing, the sense of touch, the help of other people, and other things.

When you are ready to move on, say, **The presence of light is what gives us perspective on the things around us.**

> *Note:*
>
> Be sure to thank your guest and to pray for him or her.

Starting Line

OPTION 1 (YOUNGER YOUTH)

Experience a challenge.

Set up two chairs facing one another, at least five feet apart. Place a bucket on each chair and fill one bucket with cotton balls. Ask for a volunteer. Blindfold this person and turn him or her around a few times; then give the volunteer a spoon and place him or her in front of the bucket with the cotton balls. When you say **Go,** the volunteer should use the spoon to scoop cotton balls out of one bucket and walk them over to the other bucket. The volunteer may not touch the buckets or the cotton balls with his or her hands but must use only the spoon. Stop your volunteer after sixty seconds and count the number of cotton balls that have actually made it into the opposite bucket. Invite other volunteers to participate. At some point, trick one volunteer (with a good sense of humor) by removing all the cotton balls from the bucket right after the blindfold is put on. This person will think that he or she is transferring cotton balls but will in fact only be moving air.

After the game, spend a few moments discussing how much better your volunteers could have done if they had not been blindfolded. Emphasize the importance of light and how it really is necessary for sight. When we can't see, then it is difficult for us to know whether or not we are on the right path—and hard for us to know if we're really succeeding at doing what we think we're doing.

Say, **Let's see how we can walk in the light—in our *spiritual* lives.**

· ·

OPTION 2 (OLDER YOUTH)

Discover the properties of light.

Divide the class into groups of three or four students and give each group a copy of "Properties of Light" (Reproducible 1). Ask students to consider in their groups the characteristics or properties of light and to write down their thoughts. As they are doing this, draw a similar diagram on the board. (***Note:*** If you have access to a computer and data projector during class time, you can use the interactive diagram on the Digital BRIDGES CD to show this and the points below.) After a few minutes, invite groups to share their ideas as you write these ideas within the diagram on the board. Here are some properties you may wish to include:

- The way light operates is not fully understood.
- Light travels very quickly—at about 186,000 miles per second.
- Light contains energy.
- Light produces heat—and is necessary for many forms of life.
- Some parts of light are invisible.

When you are ready to move on, say, **Let's see how Jesus Christ can provide light for our spiritual lives.** As you continue your study, encourage your students to think about how some of these characteristics of light apply to Christ.

Explore the Bible passage.

Give your students some context for today's Bible passage by discussing the following questions:

Straight Away

- **How many books in the Bible include *John* in their title?** There are four: the Gospel of John and the three epistles (letters) of John—1 John, 2 John, and 3 John.
- **Who was this John?** John was the brother of James, a son of Zebedee, and a disciple of Jesus Christ (see Luke 5:1–11). He was also known as "the disciple whom Jesus loved" (see John 21:20–24). It is possible that he was a first cousin of Jesus.
- **What other books of the Bible did John write?** John also wrote the Book of Revelation.

Read together 1 John 1:1–4. Point out the similarities in this passage with the opening verses of John's Gospel. Explain that John established credibility for the letter he was writing by reminding the readers that he was a "primary source"—someone who knew Christ personally. John had traveled with Jesus, talked with him, eaten with him, seen him die, and seen him alive again. Ask, **What was John's purpose in writing this letter?** He wrote it so that those who read it might have fellowship (a shared experience and bond) with the followers of Christ, and he wrote it so that his joy might be "complete." In other words, John's relationship with Christ was so awesome that he wanted others to share in that relationship too.

Now read together 1 John 1:5–10. Discuss the following questions:

- **Who was the original source of John's message, and what was that message?** Jesus Christ ("he" in verse 5) was the one who originally proclaimed the message: "God is light; in him there is no darkness at all" (verse 5). If we claim to be walking with God but are walking in the darkness, then we are lying (verse 6). But if we walk in God's light, then we will really experience fellowship with one another, and the blood of Jesus will purify us from sin (verse 7).
- **What did John mean about all this light and darkness and sin?** Invite students to respond. No one can claim to be perfect or to have never sinned, but when we confess our sin, then God is faithful to forgive us and to purify us from that sin. God is light and if we walk in the light, then we can see the right way to live. There is no darkness at all in God; we cannot continue to live in the darkness of sin and enjoy a close relationship with God or with God's people.

Now read together 1 John 2:1–6. Discuss the following questions:

- **There's some more "purpose statement" given in these verses. What is it? How do you think people might "abuse" it?** John said that he had passed this knowledge along to those who would read it (and we have just done that) so that they would not sin. But then he offered the encouragement that if we *do* sin, Jesus Christ is our defender. Some might take this to mean that "we're gonna sin anyway," or, "it's okay to sin because Jesus will take

Note:

For details on the possibility of Jesus and John being cousins, see the article "Jesus' Family Connections" on the Digital BRIDGES CD.

care of it." But this is not a license to do wrong—it's advice for how to stay *away* from sin.

- **How big of a "case load" can Jesus Christ the defender handle?** He is the sacrifice not only for *our* sins but for the sins of the whole world—for *all* people who are willing to accept that sacrifice.

- **How do we know that we have truly come to know Jesus Christ?** If we obey his commands (verse 3) and walk as Jesus did (verse 6). Ask your students to describe the way that Jesus walked, as you write their suggestions on the board. Students can flip through the Gospels if necessary. Jesus was humble, lived simply, helped others, shared God's love, hung out with the rejects of society, knew the Word of God, spent time in prayer, and was a man of peace. The better we know Christ, the more we will reflect these same qualities in our own lives.

- **What do you think it means to have God's love "truly made complete" in us?** Invite students to respond. This phrase is alternately translated as "having God's mature love," having the love of God "truly perfected" in us, or as "really" loving God. Even though we might make mistakes, our love for God and for others—our *intent*—is pure and godly.

Say, **God's intent is to shine his light in our lives—making the way clear for us to live a different kind of life.**

The Turn

Discuss light in the Bible.

Explain that the concept of light is used throughout the Bible. For the Jewish people of the Old and New Testaments, light was an important part of celebrations and religious services. During the Feast of Tabernacles, a candelabra would be lit. During regular prayers, the Jewish people would light candles (they still do today).

Ask a student to read aloud John 8:12. Say, **In this setting, Christ said that he himself was the ultimate light—"the light of the world." What will happen to those who follow this light?** They will "never walk in darkness, but will have the light of life."

Now ask a student to read aloud Proverbs 4:18. Say, **When we walk in the light, we will be walking on "the path of the righteous." How would you define righteousness? How do you think a righteous person should live?** Invite students to respond. *Righteousness* means "rightness" or doing right. First John told us that we can walk in the light by walking as Jesus did.

If you have time, ask a student to read aloud Ephesians 4:22—5:21. Invite class members to call out some specific ways we can walk in the light as they are mentioned. Answers may include *telling the truth, letting go of anger, not stealing but working instead, saying only positive things, not fighting, being kind and forgiving, being sexually pure, being generous, avoiding obscene talk, not getting drunk, praising God,* and *submitting to one another.* There are lots of suggestions—but if God can help us to do even *some* of these things that we haven't been doing before, then we can know we are walking in more of the light of Jesus Christ.

When you are ready to move on, say, **Jesus Christ is available to us to shine God's light in our lives.**

38

OPTION 1 (YOUNGER YOUTH)

Home Stretch

Talk about living in the light.

Ask if anyone is familiar with the words to the children's chorus "This Little Light of Mine." If you know it and don't consider it too "cheesy," recite the words or sing them together:

> This little light of mine, I'm gonna let it shine.
> This little light of mine, I'm gonna let it shine.
> This little light of mine, I'm gonna let it shine.
> Let it shine, let it shine, let it shine.
>
> Hide it under a bushel? No! I'm gonna let it shine.
> Hide it under a bushel? No! I'm gonna let it shine.
> Hide it under a bushel? No! I'm gonna let it shine.
> Let it shine, let it shine, let it shine.
>
> Don't let Satan (blow) it out, I'm gonna let it shine.
> Don't let Satan (blow) it out, I'm gonna let it shine.
> Don't let Satan (blow) it out, I'm gonna let it shine.
> Let it shine, let it shine, let it shine.
>
> Let it shine 'till Jesus comes, I'm gonna let it shine.
> Let it shine 'till Jesus comes, I'm gonna let it shine.
> Let it shine 'till Jesus comes, I'm gonna let it shine.
> Let it shine, let it shine, let it shine.

Discuss the following questions:

- **Have you ever hidden the light of God from others? Why did you do that? Were you embarrassed, afraid, lazy, or something else?**
- **How can Satan extinguish the light of God in our lives? What can we do to prevent this from happening?**
- **Do you think that God's light will shine in your life until Jesus comes? How long might that be?**

When you are ready to move on, say, **God does not give us his light so we can keep it to ourselves. God's light is to be shown—and shared.**

OPTION 2 (OLDER YOUTH)

Experience a candlelight service.

Distribute a candle to each student; the "candlelight-service-type" with drip guards will work best. If possible, turn off the lights and darken the room. Read Matthew 5:14–16 to your students. Light your own candle and share out loud a specific way that we can live as children of God's light. As you light the next person's candle, he or she should mention a way that we can live as children of the light. That person should then light the next person's candle, who will then share, and so on around the room.

After everyone's candle is lit, share the following thoughts with your students. You can do this in one of several ways:

- Ask your students to listen as you read the thoughts aloud.
- Ask a student to read the "right-hand" parts in response to your reading of the "left-hand" parts.
- Make handouts or project the thoughts and go around the room, inviting students to take turns reading aloud the successive lines.
- Play the dramatized version of these thoughts as found on the Digital BRIDGES CD.

Note:

These thoughts were sent by missionaries John and Gwen Johnson to their supporting churches during Christmas 2004.

Unclean
Outcast
Leper
Lame

> He touched them. He touches us.
> He healed them. He heals us.

Gentile
Pariah
Foreigner
Dog

> He welcomed them. He welcomes us.
> He enfolded them into his family. He enfolds us.

Sinner
Unrighteous
Rebel
Wicked

> He forgave them. He forgives us.
> He died and rose for them. He did the same for us.

The AIDS patient in Myanmar
The girl who lives on the tracks in Manila
The university student in China who claims to be an atheist
The thirteen-year-old prostitute in Bangkok
The tired and lonely businessman in Tokyo
The street vendor in Calcutta
The rice farmer in Bangladesh
The worker in Auckland who has scarcely given God a thought in the past 20 years

> He came for them. He comes for us.
> He touches, heals, welcomes, enfolds, forgives, and died and rose for them as much as he did for us.

Allow some time for your students to reflect on these thoughts. Point out again that Jesus is the light of the *world*—not some magic cure for our set of particular problems but the answer to the needs of all people everywhere.

When you are ready to move on, extinguish and collect the candles and say, **Jesus was concerned that others know how to live in God's light. So was John. We should be too.**

Finish Line

OPTION 1 (LITTLE PREP)
Put the light on!

Invite class members to pair up. Distribute a copy of "Put the Light On!" (Reproducible 2) to each pair. Assign each team one or two of the statements on the list; teams should then develop short skits that demonstrate two scenarios: one where the people are living in the light and following Paul's instructions, and the second where the people are living in darkness and not following Paul's instructions.

After the teams have had a chance to develop their skits and perform them for the rest of the class, ask, **Which of these instructions do you personally find difficult to follow?** Close the session by leading students in a time of prayer, asking that the light of Jesus Christ would clearly illuminate their paths so they can live lives that are pleasing to God.

Note:

Don't forget to distribute copies of the Portable Sanctuary to students before they go.

OPTION 2 (MORE PREP)
Create candles.

Heat some chunks of clear wax (available at most craft stores) in some old saucepans (pans that can be disposed of after this project). Use knives (butter knives will do) to shave some crayons and add the shavings to make the wax colored, stirring as necessary. When the wax and shavings are melted and mixed, pour the wax into molds, placing the wicks in the center. (***Note:*** Molds are also available at craft stores, but even sturdy plastic cups will do.) As the candles are cooling, invite students to design tags that read, *I am the light of the world (John 8:12)*. They can punch a hole in each tag and thread a piece of ribbon through the hole. When the candles are ready, they can be removed from the molds and a tag tied to each candle. Encourage students to share their candles with people who need the light of God's love in their lives.

Close the session by leading students in a time of prayer, asking that the light of Jesus Christ would clearly illuminate their paths so they can live lives that are pleasing to God.

Note:

This project will take some time. You may want to practice making some candles yourself before trying this with the group, or invite a "crafty" person to come in and lead the project.

Properties of Light

Think about the characteristics or properties of light. What is it? How does it work? What does it do? Write down your thoughts in the space provided below:

Put the Light On!

Paul gave us some specific ways to live as followers of Christ. Below are some statements that come straight from the fourth and fifth chapters of Paul's letter to the Ephesians. Work with your partner to demonstrate a situation that could occur if someone chose to walk in darkness; then demonstrate a situation that could occur if someone chose to walk in the light.

1. Put off falsehood and speak truthfully.

8. Be imitators of God.

2. Do not sin in your anger.

9. There should be no greed or sexual immorality.

3. Do not let the sun go down while you are still angry.

10. There should be no obscenity or foolish talk.

4. Do not steal but work honestly.

11. Do not be drunk—be filled with the Holy Spirit instead.

5. Do not let unwholesome talk come out of your mouth.

12. Praise God in word and song.

6. Get rid of bitterness, rage and anger, brawling and slander, and malice.

13. Submit to one another.

7. Be kind and compassionate and forgiving.

Portable Sanctuary

we love. But isn't Christmas the most important "holiday of love"? On Christmas we celebrate the arrival of Christ—his birth into this world. He came as a gift of God, the sacrifice for our sins. In Romans 5:8 Paul called this God's demonstration of his own love for us. Christmas is undoubtedly "the holiday of love," for it was out of God's love for us that Christ came.

Questions and Suggestions
- Read Romans 5:1–11. What are some other ways that God has shown his love for you?
- Thank God for coming for you, and meditate on the love that God has shown to you.

N O T E S

_____

_____

_____

_____

_____

_____

_____

Day 1
The Burden

Kathleen remembers vividly when she broke Sam's heart. She told a secret that she had sworn to keep. It slipped out before she could stop herself. The look on Sam's face when he found out about it was more than Kathleen could bear. "How could I hurt my friend like that? I'm a terrible person!" She tried to avoid Sam so she wouldn't have to see the hurt in his eyes. Finally the pressure became too great and she just had to talk to him. "Sam, I'm so sorry," she said. "I never meant to hurt you. I wish I could take those words back. Please forgive me!"

Sam hesitated, obviously struggling with the feelings in his heart. "Kathleen, I forgive you. It may take me some time to trust you again, but I do forgive you."

The burden was lifted.

Questions and Suggestions
- How does it feel when you are forgiven? How does it feel to forgive someone else?
- Is there anyone you are struggling to forgive? What is holding you back? Pray that God would help you to forgive.

Day 2
Seeing the Light

Have you ever been lost in a dark place, or been somewhere unfamiliar when the power went out or the sun went down? Have you ever had to walk somewhere in the dark, alone? Darkness is thick and enveloping. It is disturbing because something could be waiting in the dark unseen.

Darkness is often quiet and still, and sounds become amplified. What does it feel like when even the smallest flicker of light becomes visible in a dark place? Light gives the feeling of hope in the midst of darkness. Light pushes away the darkness, providing clarity and a sense of security. Paul said that before we were made alive in Christ we were walking in darkness, but Christ provided us hope by bringing light to our lives.

Questions and Suggestions

- What are some other ways to describe the good things God has brought into your life? Is it like a cool drink on a hot day? like listening to your favorite song? something else?
- Journal about walking in literal darkness and how that is similar to spiritual darkness. Now write about the difference that the light has made in your life.

Day 3
Not Ashamed

"No one after lighting a lamp hides it under a jar, or puts it under a bed, but puts it on a lampstand, so that those who enter may see the light" (Luke 8:16, NRSV).

It can be difficult to stand up for the right, especially when no one else is doing it. It's much easier to keep silent and go with the flow than to make waves. Being different draws attention—and we often prefer not to be noticed. Rosa Parks was taken to jail after refusing to give up her bus seat to a white person. Wouldn't it have been easier just to sit where she was supposed to sit? Many people around the world have been tortured because of their faith. Wouldn't it be easier just to stay silent? But that is not the calling of Christ. Christ calls for courage as we step out in faith. Our stepping out, even though it might be uncomfortable to us and cost us much, brings glory to God in heaven.

Questions and Suggestions

- Read Matthew 5:14–16. How can you be a light that gives evidence of your Father in heaven?
- Pray today that the light of your faith will shine everywhere you go.

Day 4
I Am

Moses knelt trembling in front of the bush. What would he tell the Israelites if they asked him the name of the God he had just spoken with? God replied, "I AM WHO I AM." But what type of name is that? "I AM" is really more than a name. It describes who and what God is. He exists—he just "is." At all times God is present, never changing. God reminded the Israelites that he had been the God of their forefathers and that he would lead them into the future as well. They had nothing to fear with God on their side.

Jesus also described himself as "I am." In John 6:35 he said, "I am the bread of life." In John 8:12 he said, "I am the light of the world." Bread and light are things we need in order to survive. They sustain us and give us life. And Christ sustains us and gives us life.

Questions and Suggestions

- Read the story of Moses at the burning bush in Exodus 3.
- How does God provide for your every need? Do you believe that Christ is all that you need in this world? Why or why not?
- Pray that God will give you peace in understanding that God will supply all your needs.

Day 5
The Holiday of Love

If you asked someone to identify the "holiday of love," what would that person say? How would you identify the "holiday of love"? Is it Valentine's Day that comes to your mind? We usually celebrate Valentine's Day by giving flowers, chocolate, and cards to the person(s)

Leading into the Session

Warm Up

Option 1 Discuss: Who is that person?
LITTLE PREP Index cards, pens or pencils
Option 2 Introduce something new.
MORE PREP Magazines, markers, poster board, scissors, glue

Starting Line

Option 1 Provide an introduction.
YOUNGER YOUTH Reproducible 1, pens or pencils
Option 2 Discuss being an eyewitness.
OLDER YOUTH

Leading through the Session

Straight Away

Explore the Bible passage.
Bibles, Reproducible 2, chalkboard or dry erase board

The Turn

Talk about preparing the way.
Bibles

Leading beyond the Session

Home Stretch

Option 1 Prepare your heart.
YOUNGER YOUTH Red paper hearts, string or yarn, hole punch, markers
Option 2 Experience a time of reflection.
OLDER YOUTH Paper, pens or pencils; Digital BRIDGES CD, computer, and data projector (optional)

Finish Line

Option 1 Consider some situations.
LITTLE PREP Chalkboard or dry erase board (optional)
Option 2 Wear your witness.
MORE PREP White T-shirts, buckets, fabric dye, fabric paint, rubber bands, rubber gloves, plastic for the floor, cleaning supplies

SESSION 4

JESUS: GOD WITH US

Bible Passage
John 1:1–18

Key Verse
The Word became flesh and lived for a while among us. We have seen his glory, the glory of the one and only Son.
—John 1:14

Main Thought
In Jesus Christ, God entered into human experience in order to bring us back to himself.

Bible Background

The Word became flesh and lived for a while among us. The Christmas event celebrates the incarnation of the one who makes all things new—new baby, new birth, new year, and new life.

For centuries Christians debated the identity of the Word that became flesh. Is the Word identical to God? Is the Word in some sense *less* than God? The length and sometimes the ferocity of the attempts to answer such questions expressed some believers' deeply held religious and theological convictions. Christianity's Jewish theological heritage insisted that God is one: "Hear O Israel: The LORD our God, the LORD is one" (Deuteronomy 6:4). This text, known as the *Shema,* anchored Jewish belief about God. Talk of a second divine being seemed to undercut that belief. At the same time the Greek philosophical tradition that had played a key role in early Christian apologetics took the view that God could in no way change. God was perfect in every respect; therefore any deviation from perfection necessarily implied a decline. Even the very notion of change could not be applied to God. To say that God became a human being suggested a kind of alteration in God that flew in the face of these beliefs. This confession of faith—that the Word that became incarnate in Jesus was of the same nature as God—required centuries of debate before doctrinal consensus was achieved by the Council of Nicea in 325. Even then, not all council participants agreed.

The Emperor Constantine, himself a recent convert to Christianity, convened the council because he feared that a theological dispute over the nature of the Word threatened the unity of the church, and a divided church threatened his hard-won political achievement of a newly re-unified Roman Empire. Thus he called over three hundred bishops to the town of Nicea, a suburb of the new imperial city of Constantinople, to resolve the issue. Two factions polarized the council while a large group of undecided bishops controlled the center. One view insisted that the Word—the Logos—was "of a similar essence" as God. The leader of this faction, a man named Arius, was not interested in devaluing the Logos as much as he wanted to protect monotheism and the unchangeableness of God. Opposed to Arius was the bishop of Alexandria, Athanasius, who insisted that the Logos was "of the same essence as God." Athanasius thought that Arius's view undermined the doctrine of salvation; only a fully divine Redeemer could save us and bring us to newness of life. At the end of the day it was Athanasius's view that triumphed and became the anchor of the orthodox Christian understanding of the Trinity. Most church traditions, including those who may not recite the Nicene Creed as part of weekly worship, nevertheless assume the creed's articles on the Trinity and Incarnation.

We live in an age and culture prone to analysis. The tools of scientific research have given us extraordinary analytical powers, and thus we are prone even to analyze statements or beliefs that were not intended to be analyzed in such ways. Thus we are off-track when we try to dissect the meaning of "the Word became flesh" by asking, "What was he?" The appropriate question is not "What?" but "Who?" It is the church's answer to say, "The Word was God."

OPTION 1 (LITTLE PREP)

Discuss: Who is that person?

Ask for three volunteers and distribute index cards to them. Invite your volunteers to write true short stories about themselves that no one else in the room is aware of (one story per person). The stories should be short and general (with names, locations, and so forth excluded). The volunteers should complete their cards away from the rest of the group and then swap cards with one another. When they return, the volunteers should read aloud the stories on their cards as if they are their own. Encourage class members to ask questions of the volunteers about their stories and to guess which people the stories actually happened to.

Warm Up

After you have revealed which stories go with which people, discuss the following questions:

- **What is the purpose of introducing someone?** This is how we help others get to know someone they don't know.
- **What types of information are usually shared in an introduction?** Perhaps a person's name, where that person is from, where he or she attends school or works, and so forth.
- **How well can you introduce someone you don't know?** Not very well! Point out that in the stories your volunteers shared, they were really "put on the spot" to answer questions about experiences that did not even happen to them. They may have made up some answers or guessed at them, but they didn't really know the situation. The person in the best position to introduce you is someone who knows you personally and has spent time with you.

Say, **When we know someone well, we are in a better place to introduce that person to others.**

Note:

If you have a large class, you can use more than three volunteers for this activity.

· ·

OPTION 2 (MORE PREP)

Introduce something new.

Invite students to break into groups of three or four. Distribute magazines, markers, poster board, scissors, and glue to the groups and ask each group to design some sort of new invention. Emphasize that nothing is too far out for this project. Groups can make drawings of their inventions or montages of their inventions using clippings from the pictures in the magazines. Explain that group members will need to introduce their inventions to the rest of the class, including discussing the main features and "advertising" the functions and the benefits of the inventions.

After the groups have had time to design their inventions and share the information, spend some time talking about the necessity of introductions for new products. Ask, **Why would anyone spend the time or the money to introduce a new product?** If something is new, then most people don't know about it. People will use a product only if they know that it exists and understand what it does. Brainstorm with your students about other situations where introductions are important.

When you are ready to move on, say, **When something new comes along, there needs to be a way to get the word out.**

Starting Line

OPTION 1 (YOUNGER YOUTH)

Provide an introduction.

This activity will take the idea of introducing someone to a more personal level.

Ask students to pair up. Distribute copies of "Introducing...." (Reproducible 1) and allow time for students to work in their pairs to complete the handout. They should take a few minutes to ask their partners the given questions and to write down their partners' responses. Next, give each student time to introduce his or her partner to the rest of the class. After everyone has done this, ask, **In your opinion, which introduction was the best? Why?** Perhaps one student was very creative with his or her introduction, another provided a lot of interesting information, and so forth. Point out that the purpose of an introduction is to briefly provide information that is relevant—in other words, the things we need to know.

Say, **Let's look at one introduction that was given when Christ came to earth.**

. . . .

OPTION 2 (OLDER YOUTH)

Discuss being an eyewitness.

Ask, **What is an eyewitness?** Someone who has observed an event firsthand. Invite class members to name different situations where eyewitnesses are very important. One situation in which they are very important is at the scene of a crime or an accident. The eyewitness to a crime can provide the most solid evidence in a criminal trial. Any person who has seen something occur with his or her own eyes has a lot of credibility. Ask students to share about any times when they have been eyewitnesses to important events.

Explain that as a disciple of Jesus Christ, John was an eyewitness to the life and ministry of Christ. Ask, **If I am reading John's Gospel, why should I care that John was an eyewitness to the life of Jesus Christ?** Since John was actually there in person, we should listen closely to his story because it will give us important and credible details about Jesus.

Say, **Let's look at the introduction to John's eyewitness account of the life of Christ.**

Explore the Bible passage.

Ask a student to take notes on the board as you study the Bible passage. Read together John 1:1–5. Ask, **What did John say about Jesus in these verses?** Invite your "secretary" to write students' responses on the board. John called Jesus "the Word." He said that Jesus has always been with God and that Jesus *is* God. All things were made through Jesus. Jesus is light and life to all of humankind, even though we have sometimes not understood that fact.

Straight Away

Now read together John 1:6–9. Ask, **What did John say about Jesus in these verses?** Jesus had a "witness" named John, sent from God to testify about Jesus. Point out that this is talking about John the Baptist, not the John who wrote this Gospel.

Now read together John 1:10–13. Ask, **What did John say about Jesus in these verses?** Jesus was in the world but even though the world was made through him, the world did not recognize him. He came to his own people (the Jews) but they did not accept him. But to any people who accept him—Jewish or not—he gives the right to become children of God.

Now read together John 1:14. Ask, **What did John say about Jesus in this verse?** The Word—God—became flesh and lived as a human being. John knew him in person and witnessed firsthand the glory, grace, and truth of Jesus Christ.

Now read together John 1:15–18. Ask, **What did John say about Jesus in these verses?** John (the Baptist) testified about Jesus by saying that even though Jesus came along later, he was greater than John. Jesus is an abundant source of God's blessings. Even though God had never been seen before, Jesus has made God known to us.

Ask, **How do these descriptions relate to what you already knew about Christ? Did anything surprise you? Which description do you think is most important?** Answers will vary.

Distribute copies of "Looking at His Life" (Reproducible 2) or show it as a projection. Students can complete the handout alone, in small groups, or all together. Some possible answers are as follows:

- **Give an example of Christ's being with God "in the beginning":** In Genesis 1 we see that through God's very words, all of creation came into existence. In Genesis 1:26 (NRSV), God said, "Let us make humankind in *our* image" (emphasis added). Jesus Christ—the Word—was present and active at creation.

- **Give an example of Christ's bringing light and life into dark places:** Jesus healed skin diseases, physical deformities, blindness, deafness, and internal problems; he raised people from the dead; and he cast demons out of people. Those who had little or no hope in life received hope and healing because Jesus was willing to get involved and help them.

- **Give an example of the world's not recognizing Christ:** Until he was resurrected and appeared to them, even Jesus' disciples did not understand what he had been all about and did not believe that he would return. Even today, many people are confronted with the truth of Jesus Christ—but choose to walk away from him.

- **Give an example of Christ's "own" not receiving him:** The Sanhedrin—the Jewish ruling council—sought Jesus' death because they did not accept his authority as the Son of God.
- **Give an example of the Word becoming flesh:** This was John's main point here. In Jesus Christ, God took on human form.
- **Give an example of grace and truth coming through Christ:** Jesus spent time with women, prostitutes, tax collectors, "sinners," and the sick—people who were rejected by society. While others shunned these people, Jesus loved them right where they were. Jesus saved his harshest words for the scribes and the Pharisees—religious officials who were butchering the truth of God.
- **Give an example of Christ's making God known:** Again, this was John's main point. If we have seen Jesus Christ—if we know him—then we know God.

When you are ready to move on, say, **In Jesus Christ, God became flesh and lived among us.**

The Turn

Talk about preparing the way.

Make sure your students are clear that the John mentioned in John 1 is not the disciple of Jesus and author of this Gospel but is John the Baptist. The ministry of John the Baptist was foretold in Isaiah 40:3. Ask a student to read this verse. Explain the circumstance of John's birth found in Luke 1:5–17. (**Note:** Since this passage is lengthy, you may wish to just summarize the story or read only the words of the angel. If you want to use the whole passage, you could ask each student to read a verse or a portion of the section aloud.)

Discuss the following questions:

- **What was the purpose of John's ministry?** He was to bring many people back to God and to prepare the way for Christ.
- **What is meant by "preparing the way"?** John was to introduce people to Christ and help them get their hearts to the place where they were ready to receive Christ.
- **Why do you think Jesus needed an introduction?** Explain that the people had the promise of the Messiah's coming but they did not necessarily think that it would happen in their own time. There had never before been an event such as God being born in human form—and there never has been since. Such a new and awesome thing called for a special introduction. God sent John to provide this introduction, preparing people to meet Christ.
- **Do you think John's ministry was important and effective?** Luke 3:7 mentions *crowds* coming to John to be baptized—and John made it clear that repentance (a change of heart) was necessary for baptism. At least one of Jesus' disciples—Andrew—was first a disciple of John (see John 1:35–42). Andrew brought along his brother, Simon Peter. In the Book of Acts we read that Peter went on to spread the news of Jesus Christ to many places.
- **What people have served as "John the Baptists" in your life—preparing you to receive Christ?** Invite students to respond. Parents, grandparents,

friends, Sunday school teachers, youth leaders, and others all play a part in helping to prepare our hearts to receive the word of God—through their love, friendship, teaching, support, and prayers.

Say, **Christ is waiting to enter our lives—when we are ready to receive him.**

Leading beyond the Session

OPTION 1 (YOUNGER YOUTH)

Prepare your heart.

Home Stretch

Distribute to each student a red paper heart. Students can punch holes in the top of these hearts and thread string through to make ornaments. Ask, **In what way do you need to prepare your heart for Christ?** Perhaps some students have not yet made the decision to ask Christ to live in them; others may have areas in their lives in which they need Christ's help. Ask them to write on their hearts, using markers, ways that they can prepare their hearts for Christ's work. Invite those students who are willing to share what they wrote. Be sensitive to any special needs that are expressed, and take time to pray together for them.

When you are ready to move on, say, **God came to live among us—and he wants to live within us.**

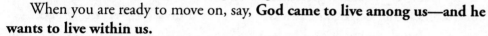

OPTION 2 (OLDER YOUTH)

Experience a time of reflection.

If you have access to a computer and data projector during class time, show the video of *A Christmas Carol* found on the Digital BRIDGES CD. Invite students to place themselves in the role of Scrooge. How have they been closed to the love of God, callous to the love of their family and friends, and uncaring about the needs around them? As with Scrooge, did it take some sort of dramatic event to wake them up? Are they in need of something right now to prepare the way for Christ in their lives?

Distribute paper and pens or pencils to students. Invite class members to spend some moments in silent reflection, considering how they can prepare their hearts for Christ. Perhaps some students have not yet made the decision to ask Christ to live in them; others may have areas in their lives in which they need Christ's help. Ask them to take a few minutes to journal their thoughts. Invite those students who are willing to share what they wrote. Be sensitive to any special needs that are expressed, and take time to pray together for them.

When you are ready to move on, say, **God came to live among us—and he wants to live within us.**

Note:
This excerpt from *A Christmas Carol* is approximately twelve minutes long.

Finish Line

Note:

These situations are provided on the Digital BRIDGES CD if you wish to project them.

Note:

Don't forget to distribute copies of the Portable Sanctuary to students before they go.

OPTION 1 (LITTLE PREP)

Consider some situations.

Read each of the following situations to your students. Pause after each and ask students to brainstorm ways to introduce Christ into the lives of these individuals. If you wish, you can write students' ideas on the board.

Situation 1

Kara has always felt unpopular and unattractive. More than once her mother has told her that her birth was a mistake. Kara's mother has also told her that she was the reason that her father left. Kara feels unwanted and alone.

How could you explain to Kara, in a relevant way, who Christ is?

Situation 2

Levon has some friends who go to church—but that has never really interested him. Only two things interest Levon—girls and basketball. As first-string guard Lavon gets a lot of playing time. Some college talent scouts have even seen him play. A scholarship is certainly on the way, and Levon can't wait to see who will give him the best offer.

How could you explain to Levon, in a relevant way, who Christ is?

Situation 3

The Christians Brianna knows are all so stuck up and self-righteous. They just don't seem very accepting. Brianna knows she's not perfect—and she can accept that fact. The Christians she knows act as if they do everything right, but she has seen them cheat and gossip and steal. Brianna doesn't want to have anything to do with those hypocrites.

How could you explain to Brianna, in a relevant way, who Christ is?

Encourage your students to think about relevant ways they could introduce Christ to the people in their own lives. Emphasize that the process of developing a relationship with Christ is just that—a process. Some people plant the seeds of ideas, others water those seeds with encouragement and support, and some are present at the time of harvest, when a person decides to live for Christ. Our role is never to force a decision—it is to introduce others to Christ and then walk the journey with them.

Close the session in prayer, asking God for opportunities to introduce his Son, Jesus Christ, to others.

OPTION 2 (MORE PREP)

Wear your witness.

For this activity, you and your students will be making tie-dye T-shirts. This is an involved process and it can be messy, so make sure you cover the floor with plastic, use rubber gloves with the dye, are careful with the materials you use, and clean up after yourselves. Make preparations ahead of time and test the process beforehand to fine-tune your skills. There may be someone "crafty" in your church who would be willing to help with this project.

Provide fabric dye prepared in pails of water. Give each student a white T-shirt or ask students to bring their own. Students should crumple their shirts loosely and then tie rubber bands tightly around them about every three inches or so. The resulting centipede-looking creations should each be placed in a bucket of dye to soak and then removed, rung out, and set out to dry. After the shirts are dry, the rubber bands can be removed. Students can then use fabric paint to write messages on the front or the back of their shirts about who Christ is to them. Encourage your students to wear their shirts as a testimony of their experience with Christ.

Close the session in prayer, asking God for opportunities to introduce his Son, Jesus Christ, to others.

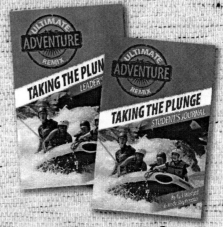

Introducing....

Ask your partner the following questions. Be prepared to use the information you gather to introduce your partner to the rest of the class.

What is your name? _____

What is the best thing about being at Bible study today? _____
_____
_____

What is the most amazing thing that has ever happened to you? _____
_____
_____

If you could do any one thing from your past over again, what would it be? _____
_____
_____

What is the most difficult lesson you have ever had to learn? _____
_____
_____

Discuss with your partner how you would introduce Christ to someone who does not know him.

Discuss with your partner how you would introduce a stranger to your church community. What words would you use to describe who your group is?

Looking at His Life

John gave a firsthand account of the life and the characteristics of Jesus Christ. Think about John's description and how you have seen these things to be true in the Bible, in your own life, and in the lives of others.

• Give an example of Christ's being with God "in the beginning": _____

_____

• Give an example of Christ's bringing light and life into dark places: _____

_____

• Give an example of the world's not recognizing Christ: _____

_____

• Give an example of Christ's "own" not receiving him: _____

_____

• Give an example of the Word becoming flesh: _____

_____

• Give an example of grace and truth coming through Christ: _____

_____

• Give an example of Christ's making God known: _____

_____

Portable Sanctuary

Day 1
Surprises

Surprises can invoke some very different responses in us. Happy surprises can leave us with a huge smile, tears of joy, and the lightest of hearts. Tragic surprises can lead to numbness, shock, and pain. Any type of surprise is momentarily stunning—our breath catches in our throats before we understand what's going on. Some people do not like surprises because they don't like the loss of control when something unexpected happens. The Israelites were waiting for the arrival of the Messiah, but when Christ came many were unaware. His presence and ministry surprised many because they didn't see that he fulfilled the Scriptures. What was your response when you learned who Christ is?

Questions and Suggestions

• Think about Christ's arrival on this earth. Who was surprised—and happy about it? Who was surprised—and became upset?
• Pray that God will help you not to miss the surprises and blessings he sends your way each day.

Day 2
In His Shoes

The best way to understand others is to walk in their shoes. Without doing that, it is practically impossible to understand the influences in others' worlds and the realities that they experience. Isn't it true that someone would understand you better if that person could live life with you for a time? It is rather amazing that God sent his Son to earth—to walk in our shoes. We can be encouraged to know that Christ understands personally the situations and challenges we face.

Questions and Suggestions

- What do you think a person would learn about you by walking in your shoes? What could you learn about others by walking in their shoes?

- Make a list of all the ways you know that God cares for you.

Day 3
Level of Commitment

A prophecy was made about John the Baptist before he was even born. A plan and legacy was laid out for his future. What if, as John grew, he had decided that he wanted to do something different? What if, as he grew, he had decided that his views and preaching were the greatest around? What if, instead of pointing the way to Christ, he pointed out his own knowledge and superiority? It might have been tempting at times, but John remained true to the calling that was placed on his life before he was even born. He kept the focus off himself and let God work.

Questions and Suggestions

- How often have you lived your own way without seeking God's heart for you?

- Spend some time in prayer, surrendering your will to God.

Day 4
Birth of a King

On April 29, 2005, the Crown Prince and Princess of Thailand welcomed a baby boy into their family. Many celebrations occurred throughout the country when the new prince was born. A procession of dancers, soldiers, a marching band, and tricycles led the way to a field where musical and cultural performances were held. Special commemorative postcards were printed and distributed. In Chinatown, lucky red eggs were given to almost thirty thousand people (a number that corresponded to the date of the prince's birth). The whole country celebrated the arrival of such a special child. How different the birth of Christ, the King above all kings—born in a dirty stable and laid to rest in a manger, a feeding trough for animals! Soft, still, and quietly Christ came, announced to only a few.

Questions and Suggestions

- What does it mean to you that Christ entered the world in such an unassuming way?

- Sing "Away in a Manger" or a favorite song of yours that talks about the coming of Christ into the world.

Day 5
The Witness

As she drove along, her mind was on the speech she had just given. It was pretty intimidating to talk in front of so many faculty members, but at least it was over now. Suddenly, as she passed through an intersection, a car slammed into her car and pushed it into oncoming traffic. She hit her head against the steering wheel. Dazed, she tried to comprehend what had happened. As she sat there, a friendly face came toward the door and handed her a piece of paper. "Are you okay? I saw the whole thing. It was not your fault. Here's my name and number. I'm late to work, so I can't stay, but I wanted you to know that I saw everything." It was good that the witness had stopped, because the other driver claimed no responsibility. The testimony of the witness was crucial.

Questions and Suggestions

- Witnesses tell what they have seen and experienced. Have you been a witness for Christ? Have you shared about what Christ has done in your life?

- Read Acts 16:16–40. How were Paul and Silas witnesses to the power of God?

Leading into the Session

Warm Up

Option 1 Play Who's the Leader?
LITTLE PREP

Option 2 Observe how something changes.
MORE PREP *Access to a copy machine during class time*

Starting Line

Option 1 Make a montage.
YOUNGER YOUTH *Magazines, paper, scissors, glue, markers*

Option 2 Consider service shown through leadership.
OLDER YOUTH *Reproducible 1, pens or pencils*

Leading through the Session

Straight Away

Explore the Bible passage.
Bibles, chalkboard or dry erase board

The Turn

Explore humility as a sign of greatness.
Bibles

Leading beyond the Session

Home Stretch

Option 1 Participate in a role play.
YOUNGER YOUTH

Option 2 Participate in foot washing.
OLDER YOUTH *Bibles, towels, basins of water, tubs, basket with strips of paper, pens or pencils*

Finish Line

Option 1 Examine the priorities of service.
LITTLE PREP *Reproducible 2, pens or pencils*

Option 2 Participate in acts of kindness.
MORE PREP *Ideas for simple community service projects; "kindness" cards (optional)*

SESSION 5

IMITATING CHRIST

Bible Passage
Philippians 2:1–11

Key Verse
Your attitude should be the same as that of Christ Jesus.
—Philippians 2:5

Main Thought
We should seek to become like Christ as we live our lives.

Acts 16 narrates the events that led to Paul's decision to cross the Hellespont, the narrow channel of water that separates Asia Minor from Europe, in response to the vision of a Macedonian man pleading for the Apostle's help. It was a pivotal decision because it meant taking the gospel of the Lord Jesus Christ to Europe. The significance of this moment was borne out centuries later when Christianity had become predominantly a European religion. A good piece of Christianity's future lay in Europe and the Western hemisphere that Europeans discovered and colonized. Those events happened long after Paul wrote his letter to the Philippians, but the Philippian church was the first that he, Timothy, and Luke founded on European soil.

Paul enjoyed the warmest of relationships with the Philippian church—a church that was the anchor of the Macedonian churches that Paul elsewhere cited as an example of Christian generosity. This warm relationship is evident in Paul's letter to the Philippians. It carries none of the sharpness of his Corinthian correspondence nor the exasperation that we find in Galatians. In fact, some New Testament scholars have labeled Philippians as a "friendship letter," but we need to understand that this phrase means more than simply friendly correspondence. In the ancient world people wrote letters of this type to their best friends as a means of influencing their moral development. A considerable body of ancient literature considers the relationship between friendship and character. Many ancients did not think that character developed on its own, but rather that it was formed positively through relationships. Friendship was among the most important of relationships and thus a principal means by which character was formed. Thus more than three centuries before Paul wrote to the Philippians the philosopher Aristotle famously considered friendship in lectures that later became one of the most famous books of antiquity, *Nicomachean Ethics*.

Paul himself tapped this ancient moral tradition when he quoted the maxim "Bad company corrupts good character" (1 Corinthians 15:33).

Out of this concern to contribute positively to the character of his friends—not to mention his brothers and sisters in Christ—Paul wrote this lovely letter exhorting the Philippians to moral growth in Christ. The first five verses of Philippians 2 are very much in the spirit of this kind of exhortation. Paul drew on his relationship with the church there in language such as "make my joy complete," and he encouraged them to develop such Christian virtues as love, humility, and a spirit of giving. Of course, our moral progress is made easier by the presence of examples, men and women who have walked before us and by their lives illustrated how we can go on. The preeminent example of this is Jesus, and it was to him that Paul pointed as the supreme example of humility in verses 5–11. Many New Testament scholars believe that these verses were originally an ancient Christian hymn to Christ that Paul quoted to powerful effect.

It is good for us to reflect on Paul's connection between humility and exaltation. It is the Christ who in all humility was willing to become incarnate that God has exalted above all others. A lowly manger and the highest throne in heaven are thus connected. We should consider the moral significance of Christ's incarnation. It was for our salvation that he came, but the Incarnation was more than a rescue mission; it also meant to show us, by example, the kind of life that God has always intended us to live.

OPTION 1 (LITTLE PREP)

Play Who's the Leader?

Warm Up

Ask for a volunteer to be *it*. This person should leave the room. Now choose one student to be the leader. When *it* returns to the room, the leader should naturally do some sort of action (such as scratching his or her head, coughing, and so forth). The rest of the class should subtly copy whatever action the leader does, without distinguishing whom they are following. As the leader changes actions every few seconds, the rest of the students should follow. The person who is *it* should watch to try to determine who the leader is. When *it* identifies the leader, the leader takes his or her place and becomes *it*. After playing a few rounds ask, **How did you keep the leader from being identified?** By following his or her directions. Point out the fact that the quicker the leader was followed—and the more people who followed—the more difficult it was to tell who the leader was.

Say, **When someone's role is a follower, that person should imitate the leader as closely as possible.**

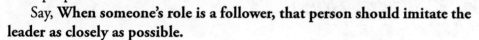

OPTION 2 (MORE PREP)

Observe how something changes.

This activity will require you to have access to a copy machine during class time. It will also require you to make a lot of "wasted" copies. If possible, use the backside of scrap paper to make your copies. If there is concern over wasting paper, you may wish to choose Option 1 (Little Prep) instead.

Take your class to a copy machine and illustrate how copies can deviate from the original. Take a page with a large amount of text or graphics and make a single copy of it. (A page from this book would work.) Show students this first copy and ask, **How close is this to the original?** Probably very close if you were careful with it; if the original was in color, then the lack of color in the copy will be a significant difference. Now make a copy of the copy, but be a little careless when doing so (start to remove the paper before the copy is complete, or set the paper crooked on the copier, or smudge the copier glass). Ask, **How does *this* copy look?** There should be more deviation from the original now. Continue to make "careless" copies of the most recent copies for as long as it takes to get a copy that is distorted and differs significantly from the first original. Over time, even careful "copies of copies" will begin to distort due to the refraction of the glass on the copier. If you wish, give some of your distorted copies to your students to keep as reminders of your study today.

Discuss the following questions:

• **Was it difficult to tell the difference between the copies and the original? Why or why not?** The first copy was not bad but as more copies were made, they started to change. The difference between any two "neighbor" copies was not great—but the difference between the final copies and the original was significant.

- **How can you tell if something is a copy or imitation?** We need to be familiar with the original and know what it looks like; then we can compare the two to see if there is any difference.
- **Why do people copy someone or make copies of something?** Sometimes because they admire that person or thing; sometimes to benefit from the original person or thing; and sometimes because that person or thing is designed to be copied, so that others can be helped.

Say, **The goal in copying something is usually to imitate that thing as closely as possible.**

Starting Line

OPTION 1 (YOUNGER YOUTH)
Make a montage.
Invite your students to divide into groups of three or four. Distribute to the groups magazines, paper, scissors, glue, and markers. Ask the groups to look through the magazines and to think about what messages the world gives them about who they should be. Invite the group members to work together to design montages that illustrate those messages. After the groups have had time to construct their montages, encourage them to show and explain their work to the rest of the class. Point out that there is really no "new look" or style that any of us can adopt—we get our ideas for fashion, music, and even speech from others, and there is nothing we can say or do that has not been said or done before.
Say, **Let's look at what the Bible says about who or what we should be like.**

OPTION 2 (OLDER YOUTH)
Consider service shown through leadership.

Distribute to students copies of "As I Lead, I Serve" (Reproducible 1) or show it as a projection. Ask students to work in pairs, small groups, or all together to complete the exercise. Some possible answers and points of discussion are given here. (If students have worked in pairs or small groups, bring them all back together to discuss their responses):

- **"The key to effective leadership is service."** Encourage students to respond to this statement. Do they agree with it? Why or why not? People usually support a leader who makes things better for them, and that's really what service is, although many people would stipulate that a leader should do what's *right,* not just what everybody wants.
- **Why does the story about Don Johnson seem extraordinary? What part do you think Don's ministry with the toddlers played in the congregation's perception of Don as a leader?** We tend to think of leaders as the "up-front" people in a church—not as helping in the nursery! This is even more true of the pastor of a large church—a person who would

have serious demands placed on his or her time and energies. But a pastor who regularly ministered to the toddlers would be perceived as "real"—connected to the people and concerned about every person in the church.

• **What does it mean that a president "serves" the people and the country? What is the measure of success for a president's time in office?** Leaders in companies and corporations get paid to do a job, and they might report to a single individual or to a board of directors. The president does get paid, but the salary is nowhere close to that of the CEO of a private firm. And the president has millions of "bosses"—the people whose votes put the president in office or remove him or her from office. So the president "serves" many people—and ideally, this person serves not for the money, power, or fame, but for the good of the people and the nation. The approval rating of a president, prime minister, or other public leader usually rises and falls on how well that person does at making life better for the citizens.

When you are ready to move on, say, **Let's look at the kind of leader Jesus was.**

Straight Away

Leading through the Session

Explore the Bible passage.
Read together Philippians 2:1–11. Discuss the following questions:

• **What does it mean to be united with someone? What does it mean to be united with Christ?** Invite students to respond. If people are united, then they live in harmony and act together; it could even be said that they act as a single entity or form a single unit. God designed the marital relationship to be one of physical and spiritual unity. If any of your students have ever been so close to a particular friend that always liked to do the same things and even seemed to know what the other was thinking, then they have experienced a measure of unity. We can have this experience with Christ—agreeing with his direction, living in harmony with his will, and acting as he would act.

• **What did Paul say would make his "joy complete"—in other words, would make him very happy?** If his Philippian friends would have the same kind of relationship with one another as they had with Christ—being of the same mind, having the same love, and being one in spirit and purpose.

• **What did Paul say was the practical way to live this out?** By being humble and considering others better than ourselves, never acting selfishly or out of vain conceit, always being sure to consider the interests and needs of others whenever we do something.

- **How do these values compare with the values of today's world?** This concept is completely foreign to many people in our society. The world says that we should look out for ourselves; we might consider others, but only if their needs do not interfere with our own. Paul did not say we should not care for our personal needs—but he said that we should factor in the needs of those around us, actually considering those people as better than ourselves.

- **Whom did Paul hold up as the example of a humble lifestyle? How did this prove his point?** Paul said we should have the same humble attitude that Jesus had. This example is extreme and should grab our attention. Jesus was "in very nature God" (v 6), but he didn't try to hold onto that position; instead, he made himself "nothing," a "servant," and willingly faced a humiliating death on a cross. Point out that execution on a cross was a criminal's death—the equivalent of the gas chamber, electric chair, or lethal injection today. *We* certainly did not start out as God's equals! If Jesus could humble himself that much and serve in such a great way, then we can humble ourselves and serve one another too.

- **What was the result of Christ's humble actions?** He was exalted "to the highest place" (v 9) and his name was made so great that every person who is now living, has lived, or will live will bow to that name and confess that Christ is Lord. Again, the example is extreme—taken from the lowest of lows to the highest of highs.

- **How could everyone from all of history bow to Jesus Christ and confess that he is Lord? What about the people who are already dead? What about people who don't believe in him?** Invite students to respond. Regardless of what people believe now or believed when they died, there will come a time when we are all resurrected—some to life and some to condemnation (see John 5:28–29). Before they enter eternity, all people—regardless of where they will spend their eternity—will finally see the truth.

- **Should we expect that everyone will know us and bow down to us if we become humble servants?** No; to expect that would defeat the whole aspect of being humble. However, we can expect that God will take care of our needs when we seek first to do his will (see Matthew 6:25–34); and if we are unified with Christ, then we can expect to share with him in the eternal joy of the glory he has received.

Say, **Christ set the example for us in living a humble life.**

Explore humility as a sign of greatness.

Invite students to look at the story found in Matthew 20:20–28. You could either read this passage to your students or ask a few students to share in the reading. Ask, **What did James and John's mother ask of Jesus?** She wanted her sons to have the best possible positions in Jesus' kingdom. Explain that those who sit right next to the ruler (especially on the right-hand side) are those who are closest to the ruler and who hold the highest positions in the kingdom (next to the ruler, of course). This "order of precedence" can still be seen today. In a formal procession, the queen or king of England goes first, followed by whichever prince or princess is next in line for the throne, who is followed by the other sons or daughters of the queen or king.

The Turn

Discuss the following questions:

- **Is there anything positive about the request of this woman?** She wanted the best for her sons. And, she had faith in the importance and the power of Christ. She believed that he would be establishing a kingdom (although she seemed to misunderstand what kind of kingdom that would be).

- **What did Jesus mean about the cup he was going to drink?** He was referring to his torture and death. When James and John said, "We can do that too!" they probably did not understand what Jesus meant, but they would both suffer for the cause of Christ. Ask a student to read Acts 12:1–2 and another to read Revelation 1:9. James died for his faith at the hands of Herod, and John was exiled to (punished by being forced to live on) the island of Patmos.

- **According to Jesus, what is the difference between leadership and authority in the world and leadership and authority in God's kingdom?** Usually, those who have power "lord it over" (like to order around) those who are under their power. But Jesus told us that to be great we should serve others, becoming as slaves to them. From God's perspective, leaders are those who put themselves last and serve others.

Say, **Christ gave his life in service of others—and so should we.**

Home Stretch

Note:

These phrases from Philippians are available as a projection on the Digital BRIDGES CD.

OPTION 1 (YOUNGER YOUTH)

Participate in a role play.

Divide students into small groups and assign each group one or more of the following descriptive phrases from Philippians 2:1–4. Ask the groups to work to create short role plays that demonstrate in practical ways the concepts found in the phrases they have been given:

- **Being united with Christ**
- **Being comforted by Christ's love**
- **Having fellowship with the Spirit**
- **Having tenderness and compassion**
- **Doing nothing out of selfish ambition or vain conceit**
- **Considering others better than yourself**
- **Looking to the interests of others**

When you are ready to move on, say, **Paul's advice in Philippians is not just some fantasy or dream—it can become a reality in our lives.**

• •

OPTION 2 (OLDER YOUTH)

Participate in foot washing.

Ask each student to take a strip of paper and to write his or her name on it. Students should then fold their papers and place them in a basket. (Don't forget to contribute your own name.) Read together John 13:1–17. Describe the process of foot washing to the class. Ask a student to draw a name and to draw again if his or her own name is selected. The student should then proceed to wash the feet of the person whose name has been drawn. Be sure to have fresh water and towels available for each set of feet. Encourage solemnity as you share the significance of this event and its meaning for present-day believers.

When the ceremony is complete, ask students how they felt about participating. Was it awkward for them? Explain that their feelings surely mirrored the feelings of awkwardness of the disciples as their Master washed their feet. Lead your students in a prayer that seeks God's guidance in finding ways to serve others.

When you are ready to move on, say, **Foot washing is one of the most humbling—and most rewarding—things you can ever do.**

Here are some suggestions for variations on this activity:

- Divide into a guys' group and a girls' group if you feel this will make participants more comfortable.
- Make arrangements to have the leaders in your group (adult or youth) wash the feet of the rest of the group members.
- If time is short, have more than one student at a time washing feet.
- For a large class, divide into smaller groups for the foot washing.
- Help to set the mood with some worshipful background music.
- Read John 13:1–17 from *The Message*.

OPTION 1 (LITTLE PREP)

Examine the priorities of service.

Invite each student to find a partner. Distribute copies of "Designed to Serve" (Reproducible 2) and ask students to spend some time completing the handout in their pairs. After a few minutes, bring everyone back together and ask those students who are willing to share some of their ideas.

Close the session with a time of reflection and prayer. Ask God to help your students as they seek to imitate Christ. Ask that God would provide real opportunities for them to serve others in their daily lives.

Finish Line

> *Note:*
>
> Don't forget to distribute copies of the Portable Sanctuary to students before they go.

• •

OPTION 2 (MORE PREP)

Participate in acts of kindness.

Prior to class, assess some of the needs of people in your congregation or in the surrounding community. Look for projects your students can do well but that will not take too much time. If the project requires additional time and needs to be done on another day, then that is fine, but a small project done right at the end of your session or immediately after church will help your students realize that they can serve at all times and in all situations. It will also enable them to put what they have learned directly into action and see it benefiting others. If the weather is cold and snowy, your students might be able to scrape windows and shovel some paths or driveways, prepare warm drinks for people to enjoy, or help the elderly find and dress in their coats after the service. If the weather is nice, you could pick up trash in the neighborhood, clean up someone's yard, or clean windshields in the church parking lot. Your students can suggest ideas as well, but you should have some ideas planned before the session begins. If you wish, prepare some "kindness" cards to hand out to those whom your group serves.

Before you embark on your project, ask God to help your students as they seek to imitate Christ. Ask that God would make your class a blessing to those whom you are about to serve.

Here's an example of a "kindness" card:

> Your windshield was cleaned today by the youth group of
>
> **ABC Community Church**
>
> God bless you!
>
> *As the body without the spirit is dead, so faith without deeds is dead.*
> —James 2:26

"During the Christmas program I couldn't remember any of my lines, and now I can't forget 'em!"

As I Lead, I Serve

"The key to effective leadership is service."

Do you agree with this statement? Why or why not? List some reasons below for your opinion.

_____

_____

_____

Read the following stories and answer the accompanying questions:

Don and Betty Jo Johnson have served as leaders in the church for many years. Don has served on a national missionary board and was also senior pastor of a large congregation. Betty Jo was an elementary school teacher for many years. All of their children have been involved in ministry overseas. When he was serving as a senior pastor, Don, alongside his wife, taught the toddler Sunday school class. On his knees, on the carpet, the senior pastor weekly ministered to small children and cared for their needs.

A pastor serves a congregation in many capacities. Why does this story seem extraordinary? What part do you think Don's ministry with the toddlers played in the congregation's perception of Don as a leader?

_____

_____

_____

In the United States, and often in other countries as well, a leader is elected every four years. The president of the United States is in charge of the executive branch of the government—a job that requires very long days, extreme pressure, and living constantly in the glare of people's attention. The president is responsible for working with Congress to form the laws of the nation. Think for a moment about the words used to describe this job: a president "serves" his or her term in office.

What does it mean that a president "serves" the people and the country? What is the measure of success for a president's time in office? _____

_____

_____

A young businessman named Millard Fuller became a millionaire by the age of twenty-nine, but his pursuit of wealth left his personal life in ruins. Convinced that God was calling him to a life of sacrificial service, he and his wife sold all their possessions and began a ministry of building homes for the homeless. Habitat for Humanity erected thousands of these homes, and in 1996 Mr. Fuller received the Presidential Medal of Freedom. "I see life as both a gift and a responsibility," he said. "My responsibility is to use what God has given me to help his people in need."

What legacy did Millard Fuller leave? What might have happened if he had chosen not to serve the poor? __

_____

_____

_____

Designed to Serve

What if you lived your life—starting right this minute—with service as your priority? How would you approach each area of your life differently? With your partner, brainstorm how you would approach these different areas if service was your main goal. Imagine that when you entered these areas, the interests of others were your first priority.

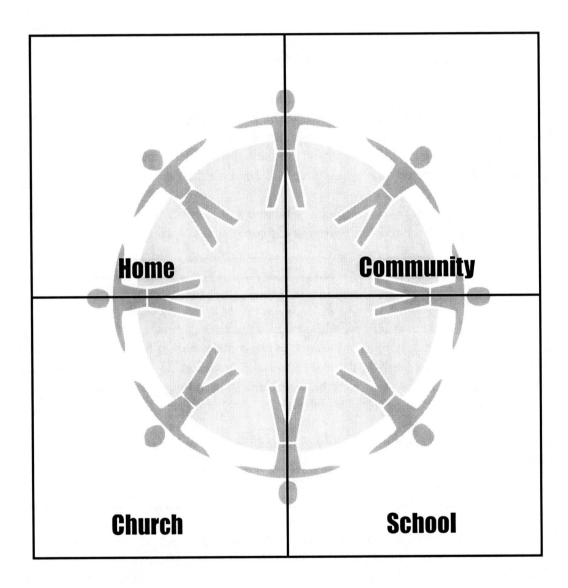

Home	Community
Church	**School**

Would this make life drastically different for you? What do you think the impact would be on you as a person? See you if can implement some of these ideas this week, making service a priority in your life.

Portable Sanctuary

Day 1

As a Slave

Although slavery is unacceptable, it still occurs in some places. In early civilizations, slavery was common. Conquering nations would subjugate people as spoils of war. Slavery often has been a source of economic benefit. In more recent history, for example, Africans were enslaved for work on American plantations. What is the difference between a servant and a slave? They both do work on behalf of someone else. A slave, however, has no will of his or her own. Christ made himself nothing and took on the very nature of a slave.

Questions and Suggestions

- How does it feel to know that Christ chose to serve as a slave? Whom was his will subject to?
- Read Romans 6:19–23. What does it mean to be a slave to righteousness? a slave to God?
- Pray that God will give you an attitude similar to that of Christ.

Day 2

Meeting the Need

In Thailand, it is an insult to point the bottom of your feet at anyone. When sitting with your legs crossed, it is important to make sure the sole of your foot is facing the floor. It is also important to remember to never touch someone's head. The head is the highest part of the body and therefore deserves respect. The feet are the lowest part and can be insulting. In the culture during the time of Christ, the feet were also considered the lowest part. During a journey they became soiled because of the dusty roads. Showing how much he really loved his disciples, Christ knelt down and lovingly washed their feet. He addressed the part that really needed cleansing. He showed how much he loved them by being willing to touch the lowest part.

Questions and Suggestions

• Read again the account of the foot washing in John 13:1–17. How do you interpret Christ's call to wash one another's feet?

• Pray that God will help you to provide that kind of service, meeting the most urgent needs of others.

Day 3
Motives of the Heart

Some people serve because they feel that if they do not do it, no one else will. They lead committees or organize events out of a sense of obligation. Others serve because they are seeking affirmation or praise. They know that they will be recognized and rewarded for their service, and they like that feeling. According to Peter, we should serve for one reason—to give glory to God. If our hearts are willing to serve, then people will give praise to God because of our actions.

Questions and Suggestions

• Has someone ever unexpectedly served you, bringing you to the point of praising God for providing help to you in that moment?

• Read 1 Peter 4:7–11. Pray that God will help you to check the motives of your heart as you serve others.

Day 4
No Compromise

When you serve God with your whole heart, there is no room for any other master. This is demonstrated throughout the Bible. Shadrach, Meshach, and Abednego walked into a fiery furnace because they would not bow to another. Daniel was thrown into a lion's den because he would not pray to anyone but the true God. Jesus turned down the kingdoms of the world and their splendor offered by Satan because he would not serve anyone but God. Christ said that even money can be a master, and those attached to it cannot fully follow God. Following God often puts us at odds with the world. In order to remain faithful, we need to be uncompromising.

Questions and Suggestions

• Have you ever found yourself in a situation where you were asked to compromise? How did you respond?

• Read Deuteronomy 11:13–21. In addition to Shadrach, Meshach, and Abednego, Daniel, and Jesus, what other biblical figures were uncompromising servants of God?

Day 5
Look for Opportunities

Mio's parents are divorced. Mio is trying her best to stay on the honor roll, but things are not easy for her and her family. Her mother is working two jobs in order to pay the bills. Mio is often frustrated because she wishes she could just have a normal life. She sees no possible way to participate in the extracurricular activities that she likes. First of all, they cost money—and second, her mother would have to find someone to help watch her brothers. Mio wishes that life could be different. She is tired of feeling frustrated and angry with her mother, but she just is. She is not sure what she can do about it.

Questions and Suggestions

• How could Mio approach her situation more positively? How could she serve? What impact could that have in her life?

• Look for opportunities this week where you can serve and be an encouragement to others.

CHRIST SUSTAINS AND SUPPORTS

Jesus is undoubtedly one of the most intriguing persons of all time. He was a man who walked humbly on earth, yet he was criticized and opposed throughout his public life. He is the man around whom an entire faith tradition is formed, and even those outside this faith tradition cannot deny that Jesus' words and teachings remain influential in our day and age. Just who was this man? The only primary documents we have are in the narrative form of the Gospels, each of which has a different bent or focus. The Gospel of John contains some of the more rich theology surrounding the person of Jesus, the Christ.

This unit will focus on some of the most direct words Jesus said about himself in John and his purpose here on earth: "Before Abraham was born, I am!" (Session 1), Jesus as bringer of life (Session 2), "I am the bread of life" (Session 3), and "I am the light of the world" (Session 4). It is our hope that your students will encounter Christ in a new way over these next few weeks. Perhaps they will learn something new about our Savior—and learn something new about themselves in the process. We also encourage you, the teacher, to encounter anew the words of Jesus and to see what they might hold for you.

Unit 1 Special Prep

SESSION 1—For WARM UP, Option 1 (Little Prep), you can use the Digital Bridges CD and a computer. WARM UP, Option 2 (More Prep), calls for a copy of the movie *Hook*. FINISH LINE, Option 2 (More Prep), requires construction paper, pens, markers, scissors, glue, and other craft items.

SESSION 2—WARM UP, Option 2 (More Prep), calls for a copy of the movie *Jack*.

SESSION 3—WARM UP, Option 1 (Little Prep), requires scraps of paper and a dictionary. WARM UP, Option 2 (More Prep), calls for snack foods such as pretzels, chips, veggies, or crackers. STARTING LINE, Option 1 (Younger Youth), requires three cans of soda. FINISH LINE, Option 2 (More Prep), calls for Communion elements (bread and grape juice).

SESSION 4—WARM UP, Option 2 (More Prep), requires a dark room and a pack of glow-in-the-dark stars. HOME STRETCH, Option 1 (Younger Youth), calls for a candle, matches or a lighter, and an opaque bowl large enough to cover the candle. FINISH LINE, Option 2 (More Prep), requires small light bulbs and permanent markers.

Leading into the Session

Warm Up

Option 1   Give orders to be followed.
LITTLE PREP   *Digital BRIDGES CD and computer (optional)*

Option 2   View a film clip.
MORE PREP   *Copy of the movie* Hook

Starting Line

Option 1   Discuss common truth.
YOUNGER YOUTH   *Chalkboard or dry erase board*

Option 2   Read about newly acquired freedom.
OLDER YOUTH   *Reproducible 1*

Leading through the Session

Straight Away

Explore the Bible passages.
Bibles

The Turn

Discuss spiritual slavery and freedom.
Bibles

Leading beyond the Session

Home Stretch

Option 1   Discuss Christ's truth.
YOUNGER YOUTH   *Bibles, chalkboard or dry erase board*

Option 2   Explore Paul's words.
OLDER YOUTH   *Reproducible 2, pens or pencils*

Finish Line

Option 1   Offer personal freedom.
LITTLE PREP

Option 2   Make reminders of the truth.
MORE PREP   *Bibles, construction paper, pens, markers, scissors, glue, and other craft items*

SESSION 1

BE FREE!

Bible Passages
John 8:31–38, 48–59

Key Verse
So if the Son sets you free, you will be free indeed.
— John 8:36

Main Thought
Jesus sets us free from sin.

Bible Background

John 8 reflects the sharp controversy between Jesus and his opponents. By the end of John 8 we see that people were ready to kill Jesus for what he had just said to them. In the Synoptic gospels (Matthew, Mark, and Luke) those who opposed Jesus are known variously as Pharisees, Sadducees, scribes, and priests. In John's Gospel these people are generally referred to as "the Jews." What are we to understand by this term? Clearly it did not have an ethnic reference. Nearly everybody in the Gospels was Jewish—including Jesus, his disciples, Mary, Martha, Lazarus, Nicodemus, and Joseph of Arimathea. We cannot be justified in interpreting "the Jews" to signify the Jewish people.

We will do well to flesh out this phrase against a backdrop that portrays Palestinian Judaism in all of its diversity. The Sadducee party drew from the priests and upper-class Jews. The Pharisees were not particularly wealthy (remember that Saul of Tarsus's trade was tent making) and were devoted to the Law of Moses in a manner that distinguished them from the Sadducees. On the fringes of Jewish community lived the Zealots, radical separatists eagerly looking for the Messiah who would lead a revolution to throw off the yoke of Roman oppression. Less well-known were the Essenes of the Qumran community. These people lived ascetically near the Dead Sea in a covenanted community, reading and interpreting the religious literature of Israel. The Qumran covenanters also had a controversy with the religious leadership in Jerusalem. Of that leadership the Essenes wrote: "Preachers of lies and prophets of deceit, they have schemed against me a devilish scheme, to exchange the Law engraved on my heart by You [the Lord God] / for the smooth things they speak to Your people.... But You, O God, / Despise all Satan's designs.... You will destroy in judgment all men of lies."[1] Clearly the Essenes were no great friends of the people whom John's Gospel later included in the term "the Jews."

Palestinian Judaism in Jesus' day was in no way a cohesive, integrated religious system. The various factions that divided that religious world had different ideas about the Scriptures of Israel, the nature of their inspiration, and the methods by which the Scriptures were to be interpreted. By the time of Jesus virtually all Jews agreed on the canonical authority of the Torah (the Law) and the Prophets (Isaiah, Jeremiah, Ezekiel, and the collection known as "the Book of the Twelve"—the so-called "Minor Prophets"). However, we are seriously mistaken if we think that ordinary Jews had access to copies of these scrolls or that all the scrolls were identical. Some Jews also read additional books that were widely regarded as illuminating the Law and the Prophets and therefore enjoyed a higher status. There eventually arose a claim that Moses had received two torahs on Sinai—the written Torah that people could read and also an oral Torah that augmented and complemented the written Torah. In Jesus' day the term *halakah* represented the beginning of that later notion. *Halakah* refers to the system of oral interpretation of the written Torah that meant to shape the everyday practical aspects of life under Torah. In all likelihood, John's "the Jews" refers to people who managed this interpretive practice and who were not only devoted to it but were convinced that it was the proper way to follow if one wanted to live righteously as a Jew. Their firm belief in this system is one of the factors that makes their dispute with Jesus in John 8 a debate about authority.

1. Quoted in Gerard Sloyan, *John:* from Interpretation: A Bible Commentary for Teaching and Preaching (Atlanta: John Knox Press, 1988), 102.

OPTION 1 (LITTLE PREP)

Give orders to be followed.

This game can be played in one of two ways. If your group is small, choose one student (someone who tends to be a good sport) to come to the front of the room. Tell this student that he or she should obey whatever you say—no questions or objections. Then proceed to give a series of various and unrelated commands. Examples include but are not limited to the following:

Warm Up

- **Pat your head and rub your belly.**
- **Stand on a chair in the corner.**
- **Run up and down the hall five times.**
- **Do ten push-ups.**
- **Give me a dollar.** (Be sure to return any money at the end of the game.)

If you have a large group, invite the students to pair up and choose one person in each pair to be *it*. The students who are not *it* get to give orders to those who are *it* (within reason). *It* should obey each order without question or objection. If time allows, invite the students to switch roles.

After the orders have been completed, discuss the following questions:

- **What did it feel like to be told what to do?**
- **Did you have to do something you really did not want to do? What was it?**
- **Do you ever feel this way in real life—that you have to do things you would rather not do?**

Encourage students to go beyond answers such as homework or chores and to focus more on their own behavior toward others.

If you have access to the Digital BRIDGES CD and a computer, you can also allow students to play the game similar to the classic Simon. This game tests the participant's ability to remember and follow a sequence of commands. Discuss how the pressure of following the sequence can lead to frustrating mistakes.

Say, **Today we will be talking about freedom—*real* freedom.**

• •

OPTION 2 (MORE PREP)

View a film clip.

Bring to class the movie *Hook* and the equipment necessary to show it to your group. The clip you will be showing will depict a man who discovers truth about himself and finds freedom in that truth.

To set up the clip, share the following information by paraphrasing it as desired:

Note:

There are no offensive graphics or language in this clip; however, be sure to screen any other scenes if you intend to show them to your group.

In the film *Hook*, Robin Williams plays Peter Panning, a successful lawyer who has no idea that as a boy, he was the real-life Peter Pan. Captain Hook has kidnapped Panning's two children, and Panning goes back to Neverland to save them. Up to this point in his life, Panning has been cold toward his children and concerned only with his job; this has been keeping him from becoming Peter Pan once again. In this scene, Panning remembers his childhood and thus reconnects with his Peter Pan identity.

You may choose either a shorter clip or a longer clip, depending on time. While the longer clip more fully sets the background, the shorter clip still captures the main point:

Shorter Clip—Start at 1:39:12, where the thimble is spinning on the floor. Stop at 1:43:37, where the scene cuts to a panorama of the tree house and the moons.

Longer Clip—Start 1:33:03 (scene 20), where Peter sees a tree with names carved in the trunk. Stop at 1:43:37, where the scene cuts to a panorama of the tree house and the moons.

After viewing the clip, be sure to explain that before this, Peter was feeling very discouraged because he could not fly or fight or crow. It was as if he were trapped. Then discuss the following questions:

- **How do you think Peter felt when he found his happy thought?**
- **What did this clip make you think and feel?**
- **How do you react when you witness someone finding freedom such as Peter did?**
- **Can you describe a time when you felt that kind of freedom?**

Encourage your students to keep this kind of freedom and delight in mind as you move on through today's session. Say, **Today we will be talking about freedom—*real* freedom.**

Starting Line

OPTION 1 (YOUNGER YOUTH)

Discuss common truth.

Discuss the following questions to help your students consider the definitions and the benefits of truth:

- **What are some absolute truths that you know—things that most people know or believe or that could be observed by anybody?** Encourage a wide and creative variety of answers, such as *I have brown eyes, the world is round, water freezes at 32° F, dry cereal is crunchy,* and so forth. As students name their truths, write them on the board.
- **Which of these things make a difference in your daily life?** Some things (such as the freezing point of water) definitely do; others (such as eye color) do not.
- **What truths bring freedom?** Encourage students to think of "freedom truths" that may not be written on the board. Depending on where your students live, their family situations, and even their status in school, they may enjoy varying degrees of freedom.

• **What is the basic definition of truth?** The truth is information that is accurate and right.

When you are ready to move on, say, ~~Let's see~~ *In a moment we will see* **what Jesus had to say about truth that will set us free.**

Note:

If you will be using HOME STRETCH, Option 1 (Younger Youth), leave these truths on the board.

. . . .

OPTION 2 (OLDER YOUTH)

Read about newly acquired freedom.

Distribute to students copies of "Fast Facts: Elie Wiesel" (Reproducible 1) or show it as a projection, and spend a few moments discussing the life and the experiences of Elie Wiesel. (Some of your students may have read Wiesel's book *Night,* an autobiographical account of his experience during the Holocaust.) Explain that the Holocaust stripped away all freedoms from the Jews who were imprisoned—the freedom to live at home, to own any property, to be with family, to worship, to eat, to have medical care, even to have any privacy.

Share the following excerpt from *Night* (also available as a projection), which describes Wiesel's first thoughts and actions after he was liberated:

Our first act as free men was to throw ourselves onto the provisions. We thought only of that. Not of revenge, not of our families. Nothing but bread.

And even when we were no longer hungry, there was still no one who thought of revenge....

Three days after the liberation of Buchenwald I became very ill with food poisoning. I was transferred to the hospital and spent two weeks between life and death.

One day I was able to get up, after gathering all my strength. I wanted to see myself in the mirror hanging on the opposite wall. I had not seen myself since the ghetto.

From the depths of the mirror, a corpse gazed back at me.

The look in his eyes, as they stared into mine, has never left me.

Note:

From Wiesel, Elie, "Night." In *The Night Trilogy: Night, Dawn, the Accident* (New York: The Noonday Press, 1972), 119.

Discuss the following questions:

• **What is your initial reaction to these words?**
• **What do you think Wiesel felt when he was first freed from the concentration camp?**
• **What does it mean to be liberated?** Liberation means freedom—release from people or things that are holding you captive.
• **How do Wiesel's reflections apply to liberation from sin?** *Do* **they apply?** The treatment of the Jews during the Holocaust was brutal and horrible— and the effect that sin has on our lives is brutal and horrible too. Liberation from a concentration camp was freedom from a terrible thing—and liberation from sin is too.

Note:

For more information on Elie Wiesel, go to http://www.eliewiesel foundation.org/eliewiesel.aspx.

When you are ready to move on, say, **Let's see what Jesus had to say about truth that will set us free.**

Straight Away

Explore the Bible passages.

Read together John 8:31–38. Discuss the following questions:

- **According to Jesus, what makes someone a true disciple of his?** If someone "holds to" (believes and practices) the teaching of Jesus. Those people will then have the truth that sets us free.
- **What kind of freedom was Jesus talking about?** The people Jesus was speaking to did not understand what kind of freedom Jesus was talking about, so Jesus elaborated: People who sin are slaves to sin. When we are freed from sin, then we are freed to enjoy life as sons and daughters of God. Knowing the truth—and Jesus brought this truth—brings freedom from sin.
- **So how can we know this truth that Jesus was talking about?** Answers may vary. Jesus himself is truth (see John 14:6). The truth that Jesus taught is recorded in the Bible, it is proclaimed in the church, and it is taught by older generations who have embraced it.
- **Why were the people upset with Jesus and ready to kill him?** They had "no room" for his word (v 37). Jesus claimed divine authority, he spoke out against the corruption of the religious leaders, he was more popular than they were, he could do things they could not, and he told the people to look for God's kingdom as a spiritual realm instead of a physical one. These ideas did not sit well with the religious leaders.

Now read together John 8:48–59. Discuss the following questions:

- **Why do you think the Jews called Jesus a Samaritan and demon-possessed?** This could have been an attempt to explain behavior that seemed unusual to them; it could have also been to insult him. (Most Jews deeply despised Samaritans, so the label Samaritan was considered a term of contempt.)
- **Why did the Jews get so upset when Jesus said that those who keep his word will never see death?** The Jews pointed out that Abraham—considered to be the father of the Jews—had died, and so had all the great prophets of old. By claiming that he could give eternal life, it seemed that Jesus was claiming to be greater than Abraham. Again, there was misunderstanding. The Jews didn't comprehend the promise of eternal spiritual life; they just took Jesus' words to be an insult, an arrogant claim to glory.
- **How did Jesus respond?** He said that it was his Father (God) who glorified him, and that even Abraham had looked forward to the day of Jesus Christ.
- **What do you think Jesus meant, "Before Abraham was born, I am!"? Didn't he mean "I *was*"? Is this some sort of translation problem?** Jesus spoke as if he were present before Abraham, just as he was present with the people at that time. This was saying much more than "I have always been around"—it was saying, "I am still present in the past." You may need to take some time to help your students grasp this concept. "I AM" was God's declaration of his name to Moses (see Exodus 3:13–14), a very simple but powerful statement implying that God exists above all things—even above

time. The Jews who heard Jesus say this would have made the association with God's declaration to Moses.

- **How did the people respond to Jesus' statement?** Their anger became so great that they picked up stones and were ready to kill him.

Say, **Jesus promised the people a freedom unlike anything they had ever known.**

Discuss spiritual slavery and freedom.

Invite some volunteers to read aloud John 8:34, Romans 3:23, and Romans 7:14. Then discuss the following questions:

The Turn

- **What do these verses say about you and me?** Because we all sin, we are all slaves to sin. Help your students understand that this is an issue for each of us—we are all slaves in need of freedom. On page 77 of his book *Blue Like Jazz,* Donald Miller states, "I like to think that I do things for the right reasons, but I don't, I do things because I do or don't love doing them … I found myself trying to love the right things without God's help, and it was impossible. I tried to go one week without thinking a negative thought about another human being, and I couldn't do it.… [m]y natural desire was to love darkness."

- **What might slavery to sin look like today?** Help students identify destructive patterns of sin. Examples could include *physical addictions, inflated self-image, poor self-image (resulting in eating disorders), sibling rivalry,* and so forth. (***Note:*** Be sensitive to students who struggle in these areas or have friends or family members who struggle in them. The goal is not to label "sinners" or even name specific sins but rather to recognize that often, sin is a string of behaviors that do not seem harmful at first but ultimately lead to a life that is less than the fullness we could have in Christ.)

- **Jesus said in John 8:36 that if he sets us free, we will *really* be free. What does that mean for you and me?** Jesus can set us free from the sin and behaviors that keep us in slavery.

> **Note:**
>
> See Miller, Donald. *Blue Like Jazz: Nonreligious Thoughts on Christian Spirituality.* Nashville, Tenn: Thomas Nelson Publishers, 2003.

Say, **Jesus promises us freedom unlike anything we have ever known.**

Home Stretch

OPTION 1 (YOUNGER YOUTH)

Discuss Christ's truth.

Invite a student to read John 8:31–32 again. Ask, **How has Christ's truth set you free in your own life? What Bible verses do you have memorized? What Bible stories are favorites of yours? What truth is there in these verses or stories that can free us?** Encourage students to share the verses or stories they know or are familiar with. As students share, write the key words or thoughts from their examples on the board. (If you used STARTING LINE, Option 1, write the words and thoughts alongside the common truths that are already on the board). Be sure to share some scriptures and stories that you hold dear in your own life. Work with your students to find the freeing truth in each example that is mentioned from Scripture. Some other verses you may want to reference include Genesis 1:27–31, Psalm 37:3–4, Psalm 121, Psalm 139, Isaiah 40:28–31, Matthew 19:26, John 3:16, and Romans 8:28.

If you listed some basic truths in STARTING LINE, Option 1 (Younger Youth), compare your two lists. Ask, **Which list are you more drawn to? Why? How are the truths from God's Word different from the truths we mentioned earlier?** Invite your students to respond. You may wish to work together to memorize one of the verses that has been listed.

When you are ready to move on, say, **When we learn and apply the truth of the Bible, we are learning and applying the truth of Christ.**

. . . .

OPTION 2 (OLDER YOUTH)

Explore Paul's words.

Distribute to students copies of "Paul's Words, My Words" (Reproducible 2) and ask for a volunteer to read aloud Romans 7:14–20 from the Reproducible. Next, ask students to reread the passage silently and to circle or underline any phrases or words they find especially meaningful. Students should then use the space provided to summarize or express Paul's words in their own words.

After allowing time to complete the handout, discuss the following questions:

• **What do you think Paul was really saying in these verses?** Paul described how he had experienced slavery to sin. He couldn't do the things he knew he should do, and he ended up doing the things he knew were wrong. Paul knew that he couldn't work this out on his own and that he needed God's help.
• **Which words or phrases jump out at you? Why?**
• **Where do you find yourself in these words?**

Invite students to share their paraphrases of these verses. When you are ready to move on, say, **With God's help, we can be free from the sin that seeks to rule our lives.**

OPTION 1 (LITTLE PREP)

Offer personal freedom.

Invite your students to spread out around the room and to sit so that they are comfortable and free from distractions. Read aloud John 8:36: **So if the Son sets you free, you will be free indeed.** Point out that your study today has emphasized freedom from sin—freedom that each of us is in need of.

Ask students to reflect to themselves on those areas of their lives where they feel stuck in sin. Explain that these areas do not need to be huge; maybe there are behaviors or attitudes that need to be changed. Perhaps there are some bigger issues, some destructive behaviors that are hurting your students and others. Again, read aloud John 8:36: **So if the Son sets you free, you will be free indeed.** Explain that Jesus has already died on the cross in order to bring us freedom from sin. The door has been unlocked for us—we just need to realize it and to walk through the door, counting on the work of Christ and not on our own efforts in order to live in freedom.

Invite your students to pray silently and to claim the freedom Jesus brings. After a few moments, end with a corporate prayer similar to the following: **Father God, we admit that we are slaves to the sin in our lives. Thank you that your Son, your truth, sets us free. Help us to truly know what it means to live a life of freedom in Christ. Amen.**

Finish Line

> *Note:*
> Don't forget to distribute copies of the Portable Sanctuary to students before they go.

OPTION 2 (MORE PREP)

Make reminders of the truth.

Ask each student to think of a Bible verse that holds special meaning in his or her life and current situation. Then invite students to write their special verses on signs or paper they can decorate using the craft supplies you have provided. Encourage your students to take these projects home and to display them as reminders of the truth that sets them free from sin. If any students cannot think of a particular verse, you may wish to direct them to Genesis 1:27–31, Psalm 37:3–4, Psalm 121, Psalm 139, Isaiah 40:28–31, Matthew 19:26, John 3:16, or Romans 8:28.

Close with a corporate prayer similar to the following: **Father God, we admit that we are slaves to the sin in our lives. Thank you that your Son, your truth, sets us free. Help us truly to know what it means to live a life of freedom in Christ. Amen.**

Encourage students who want to discuss further their freedom in Christ to speak with you personally after class.

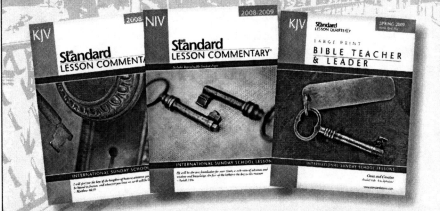

Portable Sanctuary

Day 1

Truth with Skin On

Jesus said, "I am the way and the truth and the life" (John 14:6). This is a bold statement. If Jesus is the truth, it's no wonder he can say that the truth will set us free. He knows that the truth will set us free because he is the truth that sets us free—truth with skin on. Throughout the Gospels, Jesus often prefaced his speech with the phrase, "I tell you the truth.…" Truth is his business, his concern. Why do you think Jesus is so concerned about the truth? It's because he loves us and wants to see us live in freedom. Truth brings freedom. Jesus brings freedom.

Questions and Suggestions

- Read Jesus' words for yourself in John 14:1–14. What do you think or feel when you hear that truth will set you free?
- Ask God to reveal to you more fully the freeing truth that is found in Jesus Christ.

Day 2

Remain in Me

In John 15:1, Jesus called himself the "true vine." Here is truth: if we remain in Jesus, he will remain in us, just like branches connected to a vine. Have you ever seen a branch after it is cut off from a vine or tree? Before too long it begins to wither and die. Only the branches that remain connected to the vine can remain alive and bear delicious fruit. In the same way, we can have a positive impact if we remain with Jesus—full of life and bearing fruit for the kingdom of God.

Questions and Suggestions

- Read John 15:1–8 for more on the vine and branches. In what ways does the branch rely on the vine? What happens to the branch that is cut off from the vine?

- In what ways do you rely on Jesus? Commit yourself to staying fully connected to his life-giving power.

Day 3
Father Abraham

During your last group study, you may have noticed that Abraham was mentioned. Abraham is considered the father of the Jews—and of Christians and Muslims as well. In John 8, some of the Jews disputed the teachings of Jesus. But Jesus questioned who the real father of these people was. According to Jesus, if Abraham was truly their spiritual father, they would not have been looking to kill Jesus. A child takes after his father, and Abraham would not have been looking for Jesus' death.

Questions and Suggestions

- Read John 8:37–41. What does this say about our behavior as Christians?

- How does your own life reflect the life of your heavenly Father? Pray today that God will give you attitudes and actions that reflect God's heart.

Day 4
Hard Words

In Day 3 you learned that our actions reflect the actions of our father: either our Father in heaven or—well, someone else whom we are following as "father." In wanting to kill Jesus, the Jews were not reflecting Abraham or the heavenly Father. John 8 tells us that if their true Father were God, they would have recognized Jesus as God's Son. Instead, they could not understand Jesus because their true father was

the devil. They did not believe Jesus' truth—but Jesus said that anyone who belongs to God will understand the truth. So if we belong to God, we will know the truth that sets us free.

Questions and Suggestions

- Read John 8:42–47. How do you know that you belong to God? Now check out 1 Peter 2:9.

- God calls you to belong to him. How will you respond?

Day 5
I Am!

The Jews were beginning to get angry with Jesus. He had made claims about his own heavenly Father, and they thought that Jesus was claiming to be greater than Abraham. But the truth is, Jesus is God—so he *is* greater than Abraham. Jesus said that Abraham would have been glad to be present when God's Son came to the world. Then Jesus made another bold statement: "Before Abraham was born, I am!" This made the Jews angry enough to kill him. Jesus was with God in the beginning, which makes him worthy of our praise.

Questions and Suggestions

- Read John 8:48–59. What do you think about Jesus' bold statements in this passage? How do you honor Jesus in *your* everyday life?

- For more on Jesus' place of honor, check out John 1:1–5 and Philippians 2:5–11.

Warm Up

Option 1 Read some silly laws.
LITTLE PREP

Option 2 View a film clip.
MORE PREP *Copy of the movie Jack*

Starting Line

Option 1 Discuss authority.
YOUNGER YOUTH *Reproducible 1, pens or pencils, chalkboard or dry erase board*

Option 2 Discuss symbiosis.
OLDER YOUTH

Leading through the Session

Straight Away

Explore the Bible passage.
Bibles

The Turn

Look at examples of Jesus' authority.
Bibles, Reproducible 2, pens or pencils

Leading beyond the Session

Home Stretch

Option 1 Discuss judgment.
YOUNGER YOUTH

Option 2 Discuss judgment.
OLDER YOUTH

Finish Line

Option 1 Look for where God is working.
LITTLE PREP *Chalkboard or dry erase board*

Option 2 Act where you see God working.
MORE PREP

SESSION 2

JUSTICE FOR ALL

Bible Passage
John 5:19–29

Key Verse
He [the Father] has given him [the Son] authority to judge because he is the Son of Man.
—John 5:27

Main Thought
Jesus does the work of God and brings the life of God.

91

Bible Background

This text of Scripture contains Jesus' extraordinary promise to each man and woman who hears his word and "believes him who sent me." Those who do so have eternal life and, for added measure, are under no condemnation from God. Even more than justice, the notion of judgment is the key idea in this text.

Once again we find Jesus at odds with the Jews. On this occasion Jesus has been healing on the Sabbath, in this case a man who had been lame for thirty-eight years. Jesus had found and healed him at the Pool of Bethesda. Later in the day, after the Jews had interrogated the man, he and Jesus met again at the temple and shortly afterward the Jews began questioning Jesus about working on the Sabbath. Jesus replied, "My Father is always at his work to this very day, and I, too, am working." At this saying the Jews became enraged and were all the more determined to kill him. What is it in this sentence that would provoke such hostility?

There was an interpretive tradition among the rabbis that declared that, while indeed God had rested from his creation on the first Sabbath, in one respect the Lord God had continued to labor. The judgment of the world was God's continuous and continuing work in the world. This activity was not the great and final judgment, but instead a daily judgment that rewarded and punished people accordingly for their deeds. This kind of judgment is akin to the Deuteronomistic theology that interpreted prosperity and hardship as signs of God's favor or rebuke. The daily events of people's lives, for good or ill, were believed to indicate the verdict of God's ongoing work of judgment. This line of thought may have begun among the ancient Israelites but surely they were not the last to announce that some calamity, personal or otherwise, was "the judgment of God."

Jesus made use of this interpretive tradition to announce that not only was his Father working, but so was he. In so doing Jesus transformed a debate about working on the Sabbath into a claim about his relationship to the Father and thus the nature of Jesus' authority. John 5:18b makes this quite clear, and this is important to the discussion about the nature of judgment that continues in the following verses. There Jesus declared that the Father has handed over the authority to judge to the Son. Moreover, the Son's judgment looks nothing like the judgment that the Jews had been practicing. For the Son's judgment is characterized by a generous grace; those who honor the Son simultaneously honor the Father. We honor the Son and the Father by hearing (in the sense of attentive listening with the intent to obey) and believing. Those who so honor the Father and the Son escape the condemning judgment of God, and these believers already possess eternal life in the Son.

This gracious promise does not mean that all condemnation has been eliminated. At the last day, when God's voice will call the believing dead to life, evildoers will also be resurrected. However, for them judgment will mean condemnation. Thus belief in Jesus makes all the difference in whether judgment is a thing to be welcomed or feared.

Option 1 (Little Prep)

Read some silly laws.

Share the following silly laws with your students:

Warm Up

- In Alabama, it is illegal to wear a fake moustache that causes laughter in church.
- In Baldwin Park, California, nobody is allowed to ride a bicycle in a swimming pool.
- In Louisiana, persons could land in jail for up to ten years for stealing an alligator.
- In Augusta, Maine, it is against the law to stroll down the street while playing a violin.
- A Minnesota citizen may not enter the state of Wisconsin with a duck on his or her head.
- In the state of Nevada, it is illegal to drive a camel on the highway.
- In New York State, you could be fined $25 for flirting.
- In the state of Ohio, it is illegal to fish for whales on Sunday.
- In Rhode Island, it is considered an offense to throw pickle juice on a trolley.
- In Vermont, women must obtain written permission from their husbands to wear false teeth.

Note:

This list is also available on the Digital BRIDGES CD for you to project. For more silly laws, go to www. dumblaws.com.

Now ask, **Can you think of any other silly rules? How do you react when you have to keep a silly rule?** Most of your students have probably experienced the frustration of having to follow rules at home or at school that either didn't make sense or seemed to be oppressive or unfair. Explain that laws and rules—the good ones and the ridiculous ones—are made by people in authority. There are reasons that these laws and rules were originally made, although over time these reasons sometimes become obsolete or forgotten.

Say, **Today we will be thinking about the issue of authority.**

. . . .

Option 2 (More Prep)

View a film clip.

Bring to class the movie *Jack* and the equipment necessary to show it to your group. The clip you will be viewing will illustrate the idea of a father showing his son what to do.

To set up the clip, share the following information by paraphrasing it as desired:

In the film *Jack,* Robin Williams plays Jack, a ten-year-old boy in a forty-year-old body. Jack has had a private tutor his whole life, but he is now entering public school (fifth grade) for the first time. In this clip, we see Jack as he gets ready for his first day of school.

Start at 0:20:06 (scene 2), where you see a paper boy riding on his bicycle. Stop at 0:22:16, where the school bell rings and Jack and his parents walk inside. After viewing the clip, discuss the following questions:

Note:

There are no offensive graphics or language in this clip; however, be sure to screen any other scenes if you intend to show them to your group.

- **What did this clip make you think and feel?**
- **What was Jack's dad's role in this scene?** He showed Jack how to shave and helped him feel comfortable walking up to the school.
- **Have you ever learned something by watching an adult show you? What was it?**
- **Are you the type of person who likes to learn things for yourself, or do you feel more comfortable having other people show you? Why do you think that is?**

Encourage your students to keep this kind of relationship in mind as you move on through today's session. Say, **Today we will be looking at a unique father/son relationship.**

Starting Line

OPTION 1 (YOUNGER YOUTH)
Discuss authority.

Distribute to students copies of "Who Is Over You?" (Reproducible 1). Invite class members to think about all the people who have authority over them. This could range from those directly over them (such as parents or guardians) to those who have very indirect authority (such as the president or prime minister). Other examples might include coaches, teachers, pastors, youth workers, bus drivers, and so forth. Give students time to write their own authority tree; then invite the students to share their work with the rest of the group. As original answers are mentioned, write them on the board. After everyone has had an opportunity to share, discuss the following questions:

- **What do you think about this list? Is it easy to be under someone's authority? Why or why not?**
- **How do you react when you do not like the person who is in authority over you?**
- **When is authority a good thing?**

Say, **Let's see where Jesus gets his authority from.**

. . . .

OPTION 2 (OLDER YOUTH)
Discuss symbiosis.

Explain that in nature, we find amazing examples of different species that rely on one another. This special kind of mutually beneficial relationship is called *symbiosis*. Share with your students the following example of symbiosis, either by reading it aloud or by showing it as a projection (you may wish to paraphrase it in your own words):

An example of symbiosis in nature is the relationship between the Egyptian Plover bird and the crocodile. In this relationship, the bird eats parasites that feed on the crocodile and are potentially harmful to the crocodile. The crocodile allows the bird to hunt on its body, even going so far as to open

94

its jaws so that the bird can enter its mouth safely to hunt. For the bird, this relationship is not only a ready source of food, but also a source of safety, since few of the bird's predators would try to attack the bird at such close proximity to a crocodile.

Discuss the following questions:

- **What is it that makes this relationship interesting?**
- **Can you think of other examples of mutually beneficial relationships in nature?**
- **Where do we see symbiosis in human relationships?**

Say, **Today we will look at the special kind of relationship that Jesus has with his Father God.**

Note:

For more on symbiosis, see http:// en.wikipedia. org/wiki/ Symbiosis.

Leading through the Session

Explore the Bible passage.

Read together John 5:19–23. Explain that the Jewish leaders were mad at Jesus for healing a man on the Sabbath—something that was prohibited by Jewish regulations. In this passage, Jesus was responding to their complaints and explaining by what authority he did such things. Discuss the following questions:

Straight Away

- **According to this passage, what can Jesus (the Son) do?** He does only what he sees God (the Father) doing. This includes "even greater things than these" (probably referring to the healing Jesus had just done). Also, the Son gives life to those whom he chooses, and he has the responsibility to judge us (v 22).
- **What other great miracles did Jesus do in his lifetime that would prove his claim?** He healed many diseases and problems, including internal bleeding, blindness, deafness, and leprosy; he cast out demons; he raised people from the dead and was himself resurrected; he turned water into wine; he walked on water; he was able to calm storms; and he multiplied food.
- **How closely is the Father connected to the Son?** The Son does nothing by himself but only what he sees the Father do. Whatever the Father does, the Son also does. The Father loves the Son; in fact, they are so close that when we honor the Son, we also honor the Father; or when we fail to honor the Son, we also fail to honor the Father.

Now read together John 5:24–29. Discuss the following questions:

- **What did Jesus say would happen to those who hear his word and believe in him?** They will have eternal life and will not be condemned. Also, those who are dead and hear Jesus' voice will live.
- **How can dead people hear Jesus' voice?** In this passage, "dead" refers to those who are spiritually dead. Also, without Christ we are already condemned to die because of our sin, so when we hear and believe the word of Christ, we cross over from death to life.

95

- **What do verses 28 and 29 refer to?** At the end of time, all who are dead will hear the voice of Christ and rise—some to live and some to be condemned. Point out that Jesus had just finished explaining how we can be numbered among those who live—by hearing his word and believing in him.
- **What about babies who die before they are old enough to understand anything about Christ? What about people from remote areas of the world who die without ever hearing about Christ? What about people who are born with mental handicaps and are not able to understand about Christ?** Invite your students to express and discuss their opinions about these and similar cases. Many Christians believe that children reach an "age of accountability" at which point they are able to rationally choose for or against God; prior to this time they would not be held accountable for sin if they died. Some people apply this same "exemption" to anyone who dies without having ever heard of Christ. Emphasize that whatever happens, we can trust in God to do the merciful—and right—thing.
- **What is the standard of judgment that Jesus uses?** He judges only as he hears from the Father, and seeks to please the Father by his judgments.

Say, **Jesus does the work of God—and he offers the life of God.**

The Turn

Look at examples of Jesus' authority.

Distribute to students copies of "Who Is This Man?" (Reproducible 2), or show it as a projection. For each story, invite a different student to read the text aloud; then discuss the accompanying questions together:

Matthew 8:23–27
- **What happened?** Jesus calmed a storm with his words.
- **Who reacted?** The disciples were afraid of the storm, then amazed that even the winds and waves obeyed him.
- **So what?** This story shows that Jesus has authority over nature. Refer students to John 1:1–3. Jesus was with God before the beginning of time, and he was with God throughout creation. His authority over nature comes from and through God.

Mark 5:38–43
- **What happened?** Jesus raised a little girl from the dead.
- **Who reacted?** The crowd outside laughed when Jesus said that the girl was only sleeping. The girl's parents and the disciples who were with Jesus were astonished when Jesus raised the girl from the dead.
- **So what?** This story shows that Jesus has authority over our very lives. Refer students to verse 43. Jesus told the witnesses to keep quiet about what they saw because his goal was not to amaze the crowd. Jesus used his authority well.

Luke 5:18–26
- **What happened?** Jesus forgave a man's sins and then healed his paralysis.
- **Who reacted?** The Pharisees and teachers of the Law were offended that Jesus forgave the man's sins. The crowd was amazed and praised God.

OPTION 2 (MORE PREP)

Act where you see God working.

Jesus acted only as he saw the Father act and where the Father showed him. Brainstorm with your students about where God is working in your church or community. How can you, as a class, join in a work that is already going on? This might even be through the ministry of another congregation. Maybe your group can participate in a park cleanup, sit with younger children in worship, take part in Bible clubs at school, or something similar. The idea is not to create a new program or ministry—it's to determine where God is already working and to get involved in that work. Help your students to do as Jesus did by seeking to identify and participate in the work that God is doing. You may need to make arrangements to do this activity at another time. If the activity is off-site, make sure you have the proper permission.

Close with a corporate prayer similar to the following: **Father God, we thank you for Jesus' example of working where you work and acting as you act. We acknowledge that we need help seeing clearly all that you are doing in this world. Give us the courage to step into those areas where we know you are leading us. We pray this in the name of your Son, Jesus. Amen.**

> *Note:*
>
> Don't forget to distribute copies of the Portable Sanctuary to students before they go.

Portable Sanctuary

Day 1
Seeking the Father

Jesus acted only on what he saw the Father doing. This is why he had such authority. It came straight from the Father. What does this mean for us today? Well, for one thing, we need to understand how it was that Jesus knew what the Father was doing. Jesus spent time with the Father—he had come from the Father and he set time aside, away from all his disciples and the crowds, in order to pray and seek the Father's heart. If we are looking to follow Jesus, we can learn from this example.

Questions and Suggestions

• Read Mark 1:29–39. How many people did Jesus minister to in this passage? What kinds of things did he do for them? What did he do in the morning?

• How do you take time to seek the Father and learn what he's doing? Pick a time this week to get away—even if it just means getting out of your house—in order to seek the Father.

Day 2
It Is Good

Jesus had authority over people and even nature. We have seen that Jesus received all his authority from the Father. But what kind of authority does God have? How has God used his authority? We know that God used his authority right at the very beginning—at Creation. God spoke and the universe came into existence. And God judged creation: he called it good. This is just like Jesus: Jesus has the authority to judge—and he can call us good.

- Reread John 5:19–29 as a reminder of this week's session and Jesus' authority to judge.
- Read Genesis 1:1—2:3 for an account of creation and God judging it good. How do you feel knowing that God can judge *you* as good?

Day 3
Like Father, Like Son

Do you have any Bible verses memorized? If you do, one of those is probably John 3:16: "For God so loved the world that he gave his one and only Son, that whoever believes in him shall not perish but have eternal life." Now, compare this to Jesus' words in John 5:24: "Whoever hears my word and believes him who sent me has eternal life and will not be condemned." The first verse talks about belief in the Son, the second about belief in the one who sent the Son. Belief in God and the Son will lead to eternal life. Like Father, like Son.

Questions and Suggestions

- Read John 3:1–21 to get the context of John 3:16. What are some other ways the Son is like the Father?
- Pray today that as Jesus' brother or sister, you also would reflect your heavenly Father.

Day 4
Sheep and Goats

John 5 tells us about Jesus' authority to judge. We can read more about Jesus and his judgment in Matthew where he talked about separating the sheep (a metaphor for his people) from the goats. Matthew 25:35 tells us what Jesus judged to be good—feeding the hungry and thirsty, giving shelter to strangers, clothing the needy, tending to the sick, and visiting prisoners. Why are these things good? Jesus said, "Whatever you did for one of the least of these … you did for me" (Matthew 25:40). Any time we serve someone, we serve Jesus. This is what is good.

- Read Matthew 25:31–46 for the full story of Jesus separating the sheep from the goats and judging what is good.
- In what ways do you already serve others? Pray that God will show you new opportunities to grow in this area.

Day 5
What Is Required?

The Book of Micah records the words of someone who was trying to figure out what to bring before God. The writer wanted to know what would be judged good. After offering burnt calves and other costly things (burnt calves were actually considered pretty good back then), the writer realized what God had determined to be good: "To act justly and to love mercy and to walk humbly with your God" (Micah 6:8). This is what Jesus looks for when he judges us. He looks for pure hearts.

Questions and Suggestions

- Read Micah 6:6–8. How does it feel to know that God does not require you to be perfect, but to walk humbly?
- Rewrite Micah 6:8 in your own words and meditate on this thought.

Leading into the Session

Warm Up

Option 1
LITTLE PREP
Play Dictionary.
Scraps of paper, pens or pencils, chalk-board or dry erase board, dictionary

Option 2
MORE PREP
Provide food to eat.
Snack foods such as pretzels, chips, veggies, or crackers

Starting Line

Option 1
YOUNGER YOUTH
Chug a soda.
Three cans of soda

Option 2
OLDER YOUTH
Listen to bold claims.

Leading through the Session

Straight Away

Explore the Bible passages.
Bibles

The Turn

Examine our own hunger and thirst.

Leading beyond the Session

Home Stretch

Option 1
YOUNGER YOUTH
See how God provided.
Bibles, Reproducible 1, pens or pencils

Option 2
OLDER YOUTH
Explore the concept of manna.
Bibles, Reproducible 2, pens or pencils

Finish Line

Option 1
LITTLE PREP
Share about the bread and water of Christ.

Option 2
MORE PREP
Share Communion.
Bible, loaf of bread, cups of grape juice

Bible Passages
John 6:32–40; 7:37–39

Key Verse
Jesus said to them, "I am the bread of life. Whoever comes to me will never be hungry, and whoever believes in me will never be thirsty."
—John 6:35 (NRSV)

Main Thought
Jesus is the true sustainer of life.

Bible Background

Jesus taught his disciples to ask the heavenly Father for their daily bread. Most North Americans have rarely, if ever, known the depth of poverty and need that make hunger a constant specter. Many of the world's people today live only a step or two ahead of serious hunger and in too many instances famine, while many of us own freezers that hold several loaves of bread, not to mention meat, fish, and even ice cream. We are worried about what we will eat at our next meal but not about whether we will eat at all; neither are we worried about tomorrow's meals. When it comes to food, most of us are fairly secure against hunger. But it was not so in Jesus' day. The petition in the Lord's Prayer concerning bread touched a nerve that was a daily concern of the poor and the "people of the land" who filled the crowds that Jesus addressed. Life was precarious. Except for the wealthy, who comprised a small slice at the top of the social scale, basic human needs such as food and water were not abundant, and their sources could be unreliable. Many, if not most, people raised their own food supplies and virtually all women prepared meals from scratch every day. Every drop of water they used had been carried from a well somewhere else into their homes. These texts from John's Gospel speak of bread and water in terms of such abundance as to go far beyond the dreams of many of Jesus' listeners.

Bread is the subject in the first of these two texts. Jesus had just miraculously multiplied five small loaves and two small fish (the text takes pains to point out the smallness of each) into a meal for more than five thousand, with plenty of leftovers besides. A man who can provide food in such abundance is worth following, so the crowd searched for Jesus until they found him. It is interesting that the people who questioned Jesus in this story were not "the Jews" that we often encounter in John's narrative. Here "they" were people whose questions rose not from malice but hunger, whether physical or spiritual.

They wanted bread and they wanted to do the works that God required (6:28). They were also reasonably well-informed, in that they could intelligibly refer to God's daily gift of manna in the wilderness. It was to them that Jesus declared, "I am the bread of life" and promised a satisfaction that would eliminate hunger.

The second text narrates events that occurred during the Feast of Tabernacles. This celebration commemorated Israel's wandering life in the desert wilderness during the years following the Exodus. Life in the desert was extremely hard and water was scarce there, and allusions to desert existence were frequent during this particular celebration. It would have made perfect sense for Jesus to announce during this occasion, "If anyone is thirsty let him come to me and drink." Both bread and water are in these discourses metaphors; that is, they speak of one thing in terms of another. They are signs that point to the spiritual reality of Christ's work and his gifts. Jesus referred to two of life's necessities constantly on the minds of the majority of his hearers. To talk of bread and water in superabundance was to talk of security and well-being. And that is Jesus' promise: Those who will believe on him will eat the bread of salvation and drink the water of the Spirit—and so enjoy eternal life.

OPTION 1 (LITTLE PREP)

Play Dictionary.

In this game, each player will provide a made-up definition of an unfamiliar word. The goal is to fool others into thinking your definition is correct. Depending on the size of your group, you may need to split into two or more smaller groups.

Give each student a scrap of paper. Write on the board a word that you have looked up beforehand but that none of your students will be familiar with. Now, ask each student to write his or her own definition of the word on the card. Explain that the goal is to make up definitions that sound as if they could be the real meaning. Be sure to write the real definition on your own scrap of paper. Ask a student to collect all the papers, including the one with the actual definition. The student should read aloud all of the definitions, then read through them again, pausing after each one so that students can vote on whether they think that definition is correct. After all the votes are tallied, reveal the true definition. If time allows, you can repeat the exercise with a second word. Following are some words you may wish to choose from:

Warm Up

> *Note:*
> You may wish to use a dictionary to prove to your students that you have actually given them the correct definition.

- *debouch* (pronounced dih-boosh)—to march out of the woods into an open area
- *mellifluous*—sweet-sounding
- *toggery*—clothing
- *hasenpfeffer*—a stew of marinated rabbit meat

After completing the activity, ask students how they chose the definitions they did. Some of your more creative class members may have come up with definitions that sounded better than the real ones! Explain that the goal of your Bible study together each week is to read the Word of God and to discover its true meaning.

Say, **Today we will look at some of the words of Jesus and discover what he really meant by them.**

• •

OPTION 2 (MORE PREP)

Provide food to eat.

This session will focus on Jesus' self-described role as the bread of life and the living water. In order to help students think about this point, provide some snack foods for them to eat. Choose foods that students can eat throughout the session, such as pretzels, chips, veggies, or crackers. As you share the food with your students, say, **I have given you some food to eat during our class time. Today we will talk about the food that Jesus offers—food for *life*.** Encourage your students to continue to enjoy their snack food throughout the session.

Starting Line

OPTION 1 (YOUNGER YOUTH)

Chug a soda.

Ask for three volunteers to come to the front of the room. Give each volunteer a can of soda and instruct your volunteers to chug their sodas at the count of three. Invite the other class members to participate by encouraging those who are drinking the sodas. The goal is to drink the soda as fast as possible. (***Note:*** Beware of messes. For an increased challenge, use warm sodas—they will be more difficult to chug.)

When the "chuggers" are finished, discuss the following questions:

- **Did you get to the point where you could not drink any more?**
- **How did you know when you were full?**
- **Why did you keep going?**

Explain that some people eat and drink more than others. But *each* of us has the need to eat and drink in order to live.

Say, **Let's see how Jesus can bring us spiritual satisfaction and fulfillment.**

OPTION 2 (OLDER YOUTH)

Listen to bold claims.

Help prepare your students to study some bold claims of Jesus by reading some other claims that many people would consider to be bold. After you read each statement, ask students their reactions to it. How does it make them feel? Do they believe the claim?

- **This product will help you lose ten pounds in seven days.**
- **I'm the greatest football player this school has ever had.**
- **This will only be a short quiz.**
- **This will hurt me more than it hurts you.**
- **I believe in you.**

Sometimes people claim things that seem too outrageous to be true. Sometimes their claims are appealing because they hold some sort of promise for us. Sometimes we don't believe the claims because we have seen evidence to the contrary. If you wish, invite students to share some other bold claims that they have heard. Explain that Jesus made many bold statements and claims about himself.

Say, **Today we will look at Jesus' claims to be the bread of life and the living water.**

Explore the Bible passages.

Read together John 6:30–40. Explain that Jesus was teaching a crowd of people. Earlier, he had fed more than five thousand people with five loaves of bread and two fish (see John 6:1–15). Discuss the following questions:

Straight Away

- **What was it that the people wanted from Jesus here?** They wanted to see him do some sort of miraculous sign so that they could believe in him—something such as when God had provided "bread from heaven" for their forebears. Point out the irony of the fact that Jesus had just miraculously multiplied food for these people—and yet it wasn't enough of a "sign" for them.

- **What "bread from heaven" had Moses given? According to Jesus, what was the true bread from heaven?** When Moses was leading the Israelites through the desert to the Promised Land, God had miraculously provided manna—a wafer-like substance that formed with the morning dew—as a food source for them (see Exodus 16). Jesus said that the true bread from heaven was the one God had sent to give life to the world—Jesus Christ.

- **What hope do we have in this "bread of life"?** Those who eat it will never be hungry or thirsty. Jesus will never turn us away, and he will not lose anyone in his care. We can look forward to eternal life, to being raised up at the last day.

- **Where is God's will mentioned in this passage, and what is that will?** It is God's will that none of us should be lost (verse 39), and it is God's will that everyone who looks to Christ and believes in him shall have eternal life (verse 40). Point out that Jesus did not come to fulfill his own agenda but to do the will of God (verse 38).

Note: Some students may be curious about the end of verse 40 where Jesus mentioned being raised at the last day. Jesus was referring to the Jewish belief in a bodily resurrection of all people at the end of time. The variety of passages in the Bible dealing with this topic has been interpreted in many different ways. While it is not in the scope of this session to follow this path, you may wish to direct students to your pastor or another church leader if such questions arise.

Now read together John 7:37–44. Explain that the "Feast" the people were celebrating was the Feast of Tabernacles—a celebration that commemorated Israel's wandering life in the desert wilderness on their way to the Promised Land. Any feast would naturally involve food and eating as a part of the celebration—and this particular feast was in memory of a time when the people were without their traditional source of food and had to rely on God alone to provide for them. Discuss the following questions:

- **What invitation did Jesus give here?** He invited all who are thirsty to come to him and drink.

- **What sort of a "drink" was Jesus talking about?** The Holy Spirit, which was promised to the followers of Jesus. This Spirit would be given later, after Jesus was resurrected and had returned to heaven, on the Day of Pentecost (see Acts 2).

• **How did the people respond to Jesus at this point?** Some understood and believed in what he was saying and thought, "This must be the Prophet or the Christ"; others thought that Jesus could not be the Christ because he did not fulfill the scriptural requirements of coming from David's family and from Bethlehem. Point out that this was a case of "mistaken identity" on their part, because Jesus did, in fact, come from David's family and from Bethlehem.

Say, **Jesus offered himself as the bread and water of life to those who believed in him.**

The Turn

Examine our own hunger and thirst.

(*Note:* If you chose to do WARM UP, Option 2, remind your students that you are eating to represent the bread of life that Jesus offers.)

Discuss the following questions:

• **How do we fill the different "hungers" and "thirsts" that we experience in life?** When our stomachs growl, we fill them with food and beverages; for most of us, we either get these at home or go out to eat. We fill our "hunger" for companionship with friends and relationships. We try to fill other "hungers" with money, sports, academic achievement, and so forth. You may need to help your students think in terms of spiritual and emotional needs rather than just physical needs.

• **What do we gain from these kinds of pursuits? Do they really satisfy?** Each of these things has its place in life. Jesus did not live in starvation and isolation, and he does not ask us to do so. In fact, Jesus enjoyed spending time eating, drinking, and hanging out with other people. The goal here is not to degrade friends, achievement, and these other things, but to put them in perspective. Remind your students that what we gain from these pursuits does not last for eternity.

• **How might your life be different if you sought to be filled with the bread of life and the living water that Jesus offers?** Invite your students to ponder this question. Point out that if all we do is fill ourselves on Twinkies and Mountain Dew, our lives will reflect that fact. And if we fill ourselves on Christ through prayer, Bible study, accountability, and in other ways, then our lives will reflect it.

Say, **Jesus can satisfy our hunger and thirst in a way that nothing else can.**

OPTION 1 (YOUNGER YOUTH)
See how God provided.

Distribute to students copies of "The Lord Provides" (Reproducible 1), or show it as a projection. Explain that throughout the Bible, we read stories of God providing food for his people. Invite students to complete the handout on their own, in groups of two or three, or all together.

After students have completed the handout, bring everyone back together and discuss what they have discovered. Suggested answers are as follows:

Home Stretch

Exodus 16:2–5, 11–18
- **What was the context of this situation?** The Israelites were in the desert. They were hungry and wanted to go back to Egypt.
- **What was the need at this time?** The people were hungry and didn't know where they were going to get food.
- **How did the Lord provide?** He rained down bread (manna) from heaven every morning, and provided quail (birds) every evening.

1 Kings 17:7–16
- **What was the context of this situation?** There was a drought in the land. Elijah needed food and water, so the Lord told him to go to a certain widow who would supply him with food.
- **What was the need at this time?** The woman was down to her last bit of food—not enough to provide for her family, and certainly not enough to provide for Elijah too.
- **How did the Lord provide?** The Lord caused the widow's supply of flour and oil to last until the drought was over. She was able to provide for her family and Elijah during this time.

John 6:1–15
- **What was the context of this situation?** A large crowd had come out to a hillside to hear Jesus. Jesus asked his disciples how they could buy food for the people to eat.
- **What was the need at this time?** The crowd was huge (about five thousand men, plus women and children) but there were only five small loaves of bread and two small fish available to feed them all.
- **How did the Lord provide?** When Jesus distributed the food, God multiplied it so that everyone had plenty to eat—with twelve baskets of leftovers!

Remind your students that Jesus called himself the bread of life and the living water. The people in the crowd who were talking with him would have remembered these and other stories and made the connection.

Say, **God provides for our physical needs each day—and he wants to provide for our spiritual needs as well.**

111

OPTION 2 (OLDER YOUTH)

Explore the concept of manna.

Distribute to students copies of "Beyond Manna" (Reproducible 2), or show it as a projection. Read Exodus 16:1–18 together, or have volunteers read different verses aloud. Invite students to complete the handout on their own, in groups of two or three, or all together.

After students have completed the handout, bring everyone back together and discuss what they have discovered. Suggested answers are as follows:

Exodus 16:1–18

• **What are the major points in this story?** The people complained that they didn't have any food; they wanted to go back to Egypt. God heard their complaints and sent manna and quail from heaven. Every day the people were able to eat just as much as they needed.

Joshua 5:10–12

• **What do we learn about the manna from these verses?** When the Israelites came to Canaan, they were able to eat the fruit of the land, crops that they could grow and tend. At that point the manna stopped coming. Explain that Canaan was the Promised Land. The Israelites had been traveling for forty years to reach this place, and they ate manna every day during that time.

John 6:48–51

• **Compare manna to the bread of life. How are they the same? How are they different?** Both manna and the bread of life came down from heaven, and both provided for the needs of God's people. However, the manna stopped coming once the people were able to provide their own food. The bread of life, on the other hand, will never cease. It will provide eternal life. Also, this bread of life is for the whole world; the manna was only for the Israelites.

Point out that when we take Communion together, we are portraying, in physically eating the bread, our receiving Jesus as the bread of life.

Say, **God provides for our physical needs each day—and he wants to provide for our spiritual needs as well.**

OPTION 1 (LITTLE PREP)

Share about the bread and water of Christ.

Say, **We have talked today about Jesus as the bread of life and the living water. How have you experienced Jesus in this way in your life?** Invite your students to share about times when they have experienced God's provision in their lives. Don't pressure anyone to share, but make sure the opportunity is there for all. You may wish to share a story from your own life in order to "prime the pump."

Close with a corporate prayer similar to the following: **Father, we thank you today for your Son, Jesus Christ, the bread of life and the living water. Give us understanding as we seek your provision for our needs. We pray this in the name of the one who offers us eternal life. Amen.**

Finish Line

· ·

OPTION 2 (MORE PREP)

Share Communion.

Check with your pastor or youth pastor about your congregation's guidelines for serving Communion. If someone else comes in to conduct this portion of the session, make sure that he or she understands that your teaching emphasis today has been on Jesus as the bread of life and the living water.

Read aloud John 6:51, 53–58. Explain that Communion itself will not save anyone—it is something we do as an expression and representation of the fact that we have received from Jesus the bread of life and the living water. Communion is a powerful opportunity for self-reflection and rededication; it can also be a powerful unity experience, as all participants realize their common dependence on Christ and as they commit themselves to one another. Be sure to emphasize these aspects during your time of Communion. Invite each student to tear off a small piece of bread from a loaf; distribute to them small cups of grape juice. Read aloud 1 Corinthians 11:23–26; then eat the bread and drink the juice together.

Close with a corporate prayer similar to the following: **Father, we thank you today for your Son, Jesus Christ, the bread of life and the living water. Give us understanding as we seek your provision for our needs. We pray this in the name of the one who offers us eternal life. Amen.**

> *Note:*
>
> Don't forget to distribute copies of the Portable Sanctuary to students before they go.

Portable Sanctuary

Day 1
Hungry, Anyone?

Jesus said that those who hunger and thirst for righteousness are blessed, for they will be filled. Jesus offered himself as the bread of life and the living water. He wants to fill us, to provide for our needs. When we feel empty and long for this kind of filling, we have the promise that we will be filled. It may not happen right away or in the way that we expect, but God does indeed provide. When you feel discouraged, take heart—those who hunger and thirst will be filled.

Questions and Suggestions

- Read all of the Beatitudes in Matthew 5:1–12. How do you feel when you hear that those who are needy will be filled? What other great promises are given here?
- In what ways are you needy today? Pray and ask God to meet your needs.

Day 2
Treasure Hunt

Often we try to fill our inner hunger for God with things such as money, friends, academics, sports, and so forth. These are things that will eventually go away, so what will we be left with then? Jesus understood that the things of this world are temporary, and he encouraged us to satisfy our hunger with things that are not of this world—our real treasures are in heaven. Jesus is the bread of life and the living water; he will provide for our every need. His provision may not look like what we expected, but it will always last longer than the things of this world.

Questions and Suggestions

- Read Matthew 6:19–21 for more on storing up treasures in heaven.
- In what ways do you try to fill your own hunger and thirst? Ask God to show you how to store up treasures in heaven—treasures that will last.

Day 3

Five Loaves and Two Fish

Not only did Jesus call himself the bread of life and the living water, he provided for people's physical needs with real bread. In one amazing moment, he actually fed five thousand men (not counting the women and children present) with only five loaves of bread and two small fish. We know that Jesus will meet our deepest needs if he can do such amazing things with so little. Just think what Jesus can do with us when we receive him as the bread of life and the living water!

Questions and Suggestions

- Read John 6:1–15 for the whole story of Jesus feeding the five thousand. What do you think it would be like to be one of the disciples in the story? What would it be like to be one of the people in the crowd?
- Thank God for his promise to meet your deepest needs.

Day 4

Body and Blood

Jesus declared himself to be the bread of life and the living water. But he did not stop there. We learn from the story of the Last Supper that Jesus took this a step further: his physical body was broken and his blood was spilled when he was crucified. This was the ultimate act of providing for our needs: he died so that we would not have to. Jesus truly is the bread that sustains us and gives us life in our time of need: "While we were still sinners, Christ died for us" (Romans 5:8).

Questions and Suggestions

- Read Jesus' words at the Last Supper in Mark 14:22–26. What does Communion mean to you?
- Pray and thank God for giving his Son as the bread that gives life.

Day 5

Draw Near

In John 6, Jesus made a statement about being the bread of life. He also declared that he would not drive away anyone who comes to him. Why? Because it is God's will that everyone who wants to will be saved. John 3:16 says, "For God so loved the world that he gave his one and only Son, that whoever believes in him shall not perish but have eternal life." Jesus' words in John 6 echo this. If you desire to be closer to God, you have only to draw near to him and he will draw near to you.

Questions and Suggestions

- Read John 6:34–40 and James 4:7–10. How does it feel to know that God will not turn you away?
- Thank God today that his generosity has made it possible for you to know him and to know eternal life.

Leading into the Session

Warm Up

Option 1 Discuss being scared of the dark.
LITTLE PREP

Option 2 See stuff glow.
MORE PREP *Dark room, pack of glow-in-the-dark stars*

Starting Line

Option 1 Act out Jesus' "I Am" statements.
YOUNGER YOUTH *Bibles; chalkboard or dry erase board (optional)*

Option 2 Review Jesus' "I Am" statements.
OLDER YOUTH *Bibles, Reproducible 1, pens or pencils*

Leading through the Session

Straight Away

Explore the Bible passages.
Bibles

The Turn

Discuss walking in the light.
Bibles

Leading beyond the Session

Home Stretch

Option 1 Let your light shine.
YOUNGER YOUTH *Bible, candle, matches or lighter, an opaque (not see-through) bowl large enough to cover the candle*

Option 2 Discuss being the light of the world.
OLDER YOUTH *Bibles*

Finish Line

Option 1 Commit to let your light shine.
LITTLE PREP

Option 2 Hand out light bulbs.
MORE PREP *Small light bulbs, permanent markers*

SESSION 4

A VALID TESTIMONY

Bible Passages
John 8:12–20;
12:44–46

Key Verse
When Jesus spoke again to the people, he said, "I am the light of the world. Whoever follows me will never walk in darkness, but will have the light of life."
—John 8:12

Main Thought
Jesus is the light of the world, a light we are called to reflect.

119

The theme of light connects John 8:12–20 and 12:44–46, even though their occasions differ. The first text extends the hostile discussion between Jesus and the Pharisees that had begun during the Feast of Tabernacles. In between that text and this is the story of Jesus and the woman caught in the act of adultery. Most contemporary translations of the Bible note that John 7:53—8:11 is not found in the oldest and most reliable manuscripts of the Greek New Testament. It certainly was part of the oral tradition about Jesus that circulated before any of the Gospels were written. That the story is not found in some manuscripts does not mean that it is a fabrication. Given the flow of chapter 7 into chapter 8 it does seem that the story has been inserted into an ongoing narrative.

A sharp dispute flared up between Jesus and some Pharisees at the temple during the Feast of Tabernacles. Jesus had made extraordinary claims about himself that jarred the ears of the Pharisees in the temple crowd. Perhaps it is understandable that they demanded some corroborative testimony on his behalf. Certainly this demand fell within Jewish legal tradition, which did not permit a person to testify in his own behalf or to act as judge in any case where he had a personal interest or stake.[1] The Pharisees seemed to assume that Jesus was lying about himself. "Jesus' first move is to deny their allegation that, because he has a stake in the matter, he necessarily gives false testimony (v. 13). He gives as his reason that he alone knows his origin and destiny, something his challengers cannot know."[2]

The setting of the second text is also Jerusalem, but we have advanced in time to the last week of Jesus' life. It was the Passover festival and Jesus had already entered the city in a triumphant procession. The Jewish religious establishment was determined to take Jesus captive during the Feast of Tabernacles and frustrated when their orders were not carried out. The triumphal entry only deepened their resolve to arrest him. Their opposition to Jesus was so strong as to intimidate members of their own class who were coming to believe in him. In the face of such determined opposition Jesus nevertheless repeated in much the same terms his claim to be light in a world of darkness. In a very real sense this text and the verses that follow summarize the public teaching of Jesus. From this point on he would remain secluded with his disciples until his arrest and trial. In the contrast between darkness and light Jesus stated in the most dramatic terms the difference between following him and living in the darkness of the world.

1. Cited in Gerard Sloyan, *John:* from Interpretation: A Bible Commentary for Teaching and Preaching (Atlanta: John Knox Press, 1988), 98.
2. Ibid.

OPTION 1 (LITTLE PREP)

Discuss being scared of the dark.

Ask, **How many of you are scared of the dark? How many of you were scared of the dark when you were little?** Invite students to share stories about being scared of the dark and about things that happened to them to make them scared of the dark. Encourage all students to participate. The goal is to get them talking. Your students may tend to go off on tangents from time to time, but do your best to keep them focused.

After everyone has had a chance to share stories, ask, **Why is it that kids—and some adults—tend to be afraid of the dark?** People usually like to know what's going on around them or what will happen to them. This is impossible when it's dark. Also, the seclusion of darkness makes it an ideal atmosphere for people to do illegal or harmful things; when we think about this, it can make us afraid of something bad happening to us in the dark.

Say, **Today we will be looking at light and darkness from a biblical perspective.**

Warm Up

• •

OPTION 2 (MORE PREP)

See stuff glow.

For this activity, bring to class a pack of the glow-in-the-dark stars that some people stick on the ceilings of their rooms. Make sure that they are out of the pack and exposed to the light before your session begins. You may wish to put them on the ceiling and see if students notice them before this point; or, you can hand one out to each student. Darken the room and ask students to observe the stars.

After you have impressed your students with this little experiment, discuss the following questions:

- **Does anyone know what makes these stars glow?** Chemicals called phosphors are mixed right in with the plastic that is molded into the stars. When phosphors are exposed to light, the light energizes the phosphors and excites their electrons. As the electrons lose this extra energy, they release it as a light of their own.
- **Why is it that people like light so much?** Light lets us see where we're going and it also provides heat. Don't let any of your students fool you—we all need light in order to live, whether or not we claim to like the light.
- **Why is it that kids—and some adults—tend to be afraid of the dark?** People usually like to know what's going on around them or what will happen to them. This is impossible when it's dark. Also, the seclusion of darkness makes it an ideal atmosphere for people to do illegal or harmful things; when we think about this, it can make us afraid of something bad happening to us in the dark.

Say, **Today we will be looking at light and darkness from a biblical perspective.**

Starting Line

OPTION 1 (YOUNGER YOUTH)

Act out Jesus' "I Am" statements.

Point out to your students that over the past few weeks you have looked at a few of the "I Am" statements made by Jesus. There are several of these statements in the Gospel of John.

Divide the students up into small groups, assign each group one or more of the following passages, and ask the groups to come up with ways to act out what Jesus said about himself in their respective passages. Each skit should use every group member in some way. You may wish to write these passages on the board:

- *John 6:35—I am the bread of life.*
- *John 10:7–10—I am the gate.*
- *John 10:11–18—I am the good shepherd.*
- *John 11:25–26—I am the resurrection and the life.*
- *John 14:6–7—I am the way and the truth and the life.*
- *John 15:5–8—I am the vine.*

Allow the groups time to develop their skits and to share them with the rest of the class. Afterwards, ask your students if they can think of any of Jesus' "I Am" statements that you didn't cover. Say, **Let's look at another "I Am" statement of Jesus: I am the light of the world.**

· ·

OPTION 2 (OLDER YOUTH)

Review Jesus' "I Am" statements.

Point out to your students that over the past few weeks you have looked at a few of the "I Am" statements made by Jesus. There are several of these statements in the Gospel of John.

Distribute to students copies of "I Am" (Reproducible 1), or show it as a projection. Invite class members to work alone, in small groups, or all together to look up each of the passages listed and to provide a short description of each passage. Suggested answers are as follows:

- John 6:35—"I am the bread of life." Jesus promised that those who come to him will never go hungry or be thirsty.
- John 10:7–10—"I am the gate for the sheep." Jesus said that he is the way to salvation, to rest (pasture), and to a full life.
- John 10:11–18—"I am the good shepherd." Jesus said that he lays his life down for us, he knows us, and he will not abandon us.
- John 11:25–26—"I am the resurrection and the life." Jesus said that if we believe in him, we will live, even though we die, and that those who believe in him will never die.
- John 14:6–7—"I am the way and the truth and the life." Jesus said that he is the way to God, the revealer of God's truth, and the source of eternal life in God.
- John 15:5–8—"I am the vine." Jesus is the source of our strength, causing us to bear fruit for God.

Ask your students if they can think of any of Jesus' "I Am" statements that you didn't cover. Say, **Let's look at another "I Am" statement of Jesus: I am the light of the world.**

Explore the Bible passages.
Read together John 8:12–20. Discuss the following questions:

Straight Away

• **What do you think Jesus meant by his claim to be the light of the world?** Invite your students to put this claim in their own words. The light that Jesus offers—spiritual light—is offered to all peoples of the world, to anyone who will accept and follow that light. This light is not just for seeing or for heat, but it's the light of life—*eternal* life.

• **Why did the Pharisees tell Jesus that his words were not valid?** They said that he was appearing as his own witness—in other words, he was just vouching for himself. Today we would typically hear this sort of challenge in a negative way: if a person were accused of stealing something and said, "I saw myself, and I didn't do it!" we would not give much credit to that testimony. The Pharisees were basically saying, "You're saying these things about yourself—why should we believe you?"

• **How did Jesus answer the objection of the Pharisees?** He said, "I do have another witness—the Father who sent me."

• **How did the Pharisees respond to Jesus' response?** They did not understand who his father was.

• **What strikes you about Jesus' words here?** Invite students to respond. Point out that Jesus had a very clear picture of who his Father was and what his purpose was.

• **What do we learn about Jesus' relationship with his Father?** Jesus' words are as good as his Father's—and vice versa. Jesus is very close to his Father.

Now read together John 12:44–46. Discuss the following questions:

• **According to Jesus, what happens when we believe in him?** When we believe in Christ, we believe in his Father, God, as well—it's a package deal. When we look at Christ, we see God. And when we believe in Christ, we leave the darkness behind and come into the light.

• **Why do you think Jesus "cried out" (shouted) these words?** Invite students to respond. According to verses 37–43, many people had still refused to believe in Jesus, even after he had done many miraculous things. (Moving backward through the Gospel of John, Jesus had raised Lazarus from the dead, healed a man who was blind, multiplied food to feed thousands, healed a boy who was sick, demonstrated miraculous knowledge of a Samaritan woman's life, and changed water to wine.) There were some leaders who believed in Jesus but would not act on their belief for fear of what others would think (verses 42–43). Jesus may have felt frustration at this or may have spoken so that people would be sure to hear him and know the importance of what he was saying.

Say, **Jesus identified himself as the light of the world.**

The Turn

Discuss walking in the light.

Explain that Jesus' teaching on being the light of the world impacted John so much that he himself reflected on it and taught about it later. Invite a student volunteer to read 1 John 1:5–7 and 2:9–11 aloud. Discuss the following questions:

- **Why is light useful when we are walking?** Light illumines our path and shows us where to go. Help your students to understand that this is also true in our spiritual lives—if we're seeking God and trying to do what God wants, we need the light of God to show us the way. When we walk around in the dark (even in the "spiritual dark"), we run into things, stumble, fall, and hurt ourselves.
- **How could anyone claim to have fellowship with God but not really have that fellowship?** Your students will possibly be aware of people who attend church faithfully but fail to live out their faith during the rest of the week. This may be an issue with your group in general or with some individual students. John presented the situation almost as something ridiculous—not the norm, not the way it should be! Our lives should clearly indicate that we have a relationship with God.
- **What benefits do we have when we walk in the light of God?** According to John, we will have fellowship (close and authentic relationships) with one another and be purified from sin.
- **What is one way that John specifically defined "walking in the darkness"?** By hating our brothers (and sisters). If we live with hatred, then we cannot claim to be walking in the light of God.
- **How might this change the way you and I live today? What are some ways we could put John's words into practice?** Invite students to respond.

Say, **John understood how much we need the light of Jesus in our lives.**

OPTION 1 (YOUNGER YOUTH)

Let your light shine.

Distribute to students copies of "Lamps and Cities" (Reproducible 2), or show it as a projection. Invite a student to read aloud Matthew 5:14–16. Explain that in these verses, Jesus said that our lives are light. Up to this point you have discussed how Jesus is the light of God in our lives. But if we walk with Jesus, then we also are the light of the world.

Light a candle and set it on a table, then cover the lit candle with an opaque bowl. (If possible, dim the lights in the room.) Explain that this is a picture of our lives when we live in fear or shame. The light is diminished and ineffective, and if covered tightly enough it will go out due to lack of oxygen. Now uncover the candle (and relight it if necessary). Discuss the following questions:

Home Stretch

- **Why should we let the light of our lives shine?** So that people will see the good that we do and praise God because of it. Point out that there's no pride or glory involved in this kind of "shining"—it's all for God's glory.
- **Would anyone realistically expect that a city on a hill could be hidden, or that someone would light a lamp and put it under a bowl?** No; these examples would have probably made Jesus' listeners laugh at their absurdity. Ask your students if they have ever been in a plane or in the mountains at night and looked down on a city. Even a small city can be seen because of the light! And a lamp under a bowl does absolutely no good; it wastes energy and gives no light to anyone.
- **What are some real ways that we can let the light of God shine in us, so that others might be drawn to God?** Invite your students to reflect on their handouts and to share their thoughts. Make sure your students understand that shining for God is not some sort of checklist that we complete. A lamp is a continuously burning source. God's love should shine through us constantly so that wherever we are and whatever we do, others will be drawn to God, the source.

When you are ready to move on, say, **God asks you to be a city on a hill, shining for his glory.**

Note:

Experiment beforehand with your opaque bowl. If there is a melting problem, you may wish to use a stainless steel bowl instead. And don't forget to extinguish your candle before your session is done!

OPTION 2 (OLDER YOUTH)

Discuss being the light of the world.

Invite a student to read aloud Matthew 5:14–16. Discuss the following questions:

- **What key difference is there between the use of the metaphor of light in John's writings and here in the Gospel of Matthew?** In John, Jesus declared that he was the light of the world; in Matthew, we see that we are also called to be the light of the world.

125

- **What does this say about our relationship with Jesus?** The relationship should be so close that we take on Jesus' characteristics, becoming more and more like him.
- **What do you think Jesus meant by the image of a city on a hill?** Ask your students if they have ever been in a plane or in the mountains at night and looked down on a city. Even a small city can be seen because of the light! It would be ridiculous to expect a city on a hill to be hidden.
- **What do you think Jesus meant by the image of a lamp under a bowl?** A lamp under a bowl does absolutely no good; it wastes energy and gives no light to anyone. Again, it would be ridiculous to expect anyone to do this. A city on a hill will be seen, and a lamp, by its very nature, is *designed* to be seen by others.
- **What are some real ways that we can let the light of God shine in us, so that others might be drawn to God?** Invite your students to respond. Make sure they understand that shining for God is not some sort of checklist we complete. A lamp is a continuously burning source. God's love should shine through us constantly so that wherever we are and whatever we do, others will be drawn to God, the source.

When you are ready to move on, say, **God asks you to be a city on a hill, shining for his glory.**

Finish Line

OPTION 1 (LITTLE PREP)
Commit to let your light shine.
Ask each student to think of one of the specific ways to let God's light shine in his or her life. Encourage class members to think in terms of their own contexts—school, sports, family, friends, and so forth. Emphasize the following points:

- **Being a light for God is not dependent on personality.** You don't have to be the most outgoing, popular person in school in order to shine for Christ. God gives each of us different gifts and characteristics and he works through those to shine his light in our lives.
- **Being a light for God is not necessarily an up-front thing.** You don't need to stand up on a cafeteria table at lunch time and sing "Amazing Grace." God can bless others through the ordinary, everyday conversations you have with them.
- **Being a light for God is not a one-time thing.** Just saying to someone "God loves you" is not going to shine much light! But to back up those words by praying for people, by showing them kindness and patience, and by being there for them day after day will present God's light as a consistent source they can follow.

Close with a corporate prayer similar to the following: **Father, we thank you that Jesus is the light of the world that shines into the darkest places. Help us to reflect that light in everything we do. Reveal opportunities for us to be a light to others. We pray these things in the name of your Son, Jesus. Amen.**

Note:

Don't forget to distribute copies of the Portable Sanctuary to students before they go.

OPTION 2 (MORE PREP)

Hand out light bulbs.

Bring to class some small light bulbs and give one to each student. (**Note:** If there is another activity after this session and you feel that the light bulbs will be distracting there, or if you are worried that students will purposely break the bulbs, use Option 1 instead.) If you plan ahead, you can save up old bulbs; if possible, you can get a variety of types of bulbs to represent the differences in your students. Invite students to use permanent markers to write on their bulbs some short phrases that will remind them of today's session. Possible phrases include:

- *I have come into the world as a light.*
- *Let your light shine before others.*
- *You are the light of the world.*

Emphasize that being a light for God is not dependent on personality; God gives each of us different gifts and characteristics and he works through those to shine his light in our lives. Also, being a light for God is not necessarily an up-front thing. God can bless others through the ordinary, everyday conversations we have with them. And being a light for God is not a one-time thing. When we consistently pray for people, show them kindness and patience, and are there for them day after day, we present God's light as a source they can follow.

Close with a corporate prayer similar to the following: **Father, we thank you that Jesus is the light of the world that shines into the darkest places. Help us to reflect that light in everything we do. Reveal opportunities for us to be a light to others. We pray these things in the name of your Son, Jesus. Amen.**

> *Note:*
>
> Don't forget to distribute copies of the Portable Sanctuary to students before they go.

127

Portable Sanctuary

Day 1
A Lamp for My Path

You may have heard the words of Psalm 119:105: "Your word is a lamp to my feet and a light for my path." But have you thought about what this means if we read it knowing that Jesus is the light of the world? We are called to walk in the light, and this verse tells us that one way to be in the light is by staying close to God's Word, allowing it to illuminate our way. We also know that Jesus is the Word (see John 1:1). It gives a whole new meaning to "walk in the light," doesn't it?

Questions and Suggestions

- Read 1 John 1:5–7. What is one way you can walk in the light this week?

- Here are some good ways to use God's Word to help you walk in the light: memorize a verse, commit to reading an entire book of the Bible, or write out a favorite verse and post it in a place you will see it often.

Day 2
Sun Spots

The Book of Revelation paints a beautiful picture of what heaven (the New Jerusalem) will be like. Along with other detailed descriptions, we are told there is no sun or moon in that city because "the glory of God gives it light, and the Lamb is its lamp" (Revelation 21:23). Jesus is the light of the world, and this is only a reflection of the great light that is in heaven because of God's glory. If we are the light of the world, we also reflect a piece of that glory.

NOTES

- Read Revelation 21:15–27 for a fuller description of the New Jerusalem. If want a real challenge, read the entire Book of Revelation. You may find it quite interesting.
- How does it feel to think that you are a reflection of God's glory?

Day 3
Fire and Cloud

Did you know that "light" is a common metaphor not only for Jesus, but for God as well? When Moses led the Israelites out of Egypt, they were in need of a guide for their forty-year trek in the desert. So God led them as a cloud by day and a pillar of fire by night. There was no need for flashlights! God was their light source at night. People listening to Jesus' claim to be "the light of the world" may have remembered this story and understood the nature of Jesus' relationship to God.

Questions and Suggestions

- Read Exodus 13:17–22 for the story of the cloud and the pillar of fire.
- How do you think God as a pillar of fire, lighting the path for the Israelites, relates to Psalm 119:105: "Your word is a lamp to my feet and a light for my path"?

Day 4
In The Beginning

"In the beginning was the Word, and the Word was with God, and the Word was God" (John 1:1). These words introduce the Gospel of John, telling us about Jesus. We are told that "in him was life, and that life was the light of [people]" (John 1:4). Jesus was present and active before time began, in the beginning. So when Jesus says he is the light of the world, we know that this is an eternal light, the light that has infused all things with God's light since the beginning of time.

- Read John 1:1–18, sometimes called the prologue to the Gospel of John, and pay close attention to any references to light and dark. How did John use light and dark to illustrate the nature of Christ and the relationship of human beings to Christ?
- Where do you see traces of light and dark in your own life? Ask God to make you shine brightly for his glory.

Day 5
Let There Be Light

When God made the universe, what was the first thing created? Light. God created light and separated the light from the darkness, naming them day and night. This is just one more example of a reference to light and dark in the Bible. It is interesting to think that light was the first thing God created—and Jesus, who was with God in the beginning, is called the light of the world. We do not know exactly how these two things are specifically connected, but it's worth thinking about.

Questions and Suggestions

- Read the story of creation in Genesis 1:1—2:3. Pay attention to the role of light. How do you think the creation of light is connected with Jesus as the light of the world?
- Thank God that you can count on his light to guide you—now and forever.

CHRIST GUIDES AND PROTECTS

This unit will provide further insight into the work of Jesus Christ by continuing on with the "I am" sayings in the Gospel of John. These sessions particularly focus on Jesus' relationship to Christians from a corporate perspective. The modern-day embrace of capitalism and individualism in North America makes this perspective even more important for us to see. So much of the ongoing work of Christ is done through the people of the church—the body of Christ, the hands and feet of Christ. If someone says "Christ guides and protects," he or she probably means, "Christ guides and protects *me*." But this reduces the Savior to an insurance plan—good for safe travels or for help finding a new job. When we journey with other Christian pilgrims on the road of life—and allow them to share our own journeys with us—then we experience more fully the guidance and protection of Christ, the way he intended it to be.

Session 1 will examine the role of Jesus as the good shepherd of the flock. Session 2 will explore Jesus' role as the resurrection and the life. Session 3 will look at Jesus as the way, the truth, and the life. Session 4 will study how we can tap into the life of Jesus, the true vine.

Jesus Christ, the good shepherd, has conquered death and is the way to the Father—if we will remain connected to the vine.

Unit 3 Special Prep

SESSION 1—WARM UP, Option 2 (More Prep), calls for a recording of famous voices. STARTING LINE, Option 1 (Younger Youth), requires Disc 2 of *The Incredibles* DVD. FINISH LINE, Option 2 (More Prep), calls for information cards and the time and equipment necessary to communicate with your students during the week.

SESSION 2—WARM UP, Option 2 (More Prep), requires the obituary section of a newspaper. HOME STRETCH, Option 2 (Older Youth), calls for *The Matrix* DVD. FINISH LINE, Option 2 (More Prep), requires a trip to a local cemetery.

SESSION 3—For WARM UP, Option 1 (Little Prep), you can use candy or another small prize. WARM UP, Option 2 (More Prep), calls for pictures of a big house, or a trip to see one.

SESSION 4—WARM UP, Option 2 (More Prep), requires a piece of fruit for each student, and paper bags. HOME STRETCH, Option 2 (Older Youth), calls for a set of pruning shears; you can also use some branches (preferably live) to prune. FINISH LINE, Option 2 (More Prep), requires some small vine shoots.

Leading into the Session

Warm Up

Option 1 Discuss the importance of listening.
LITTLE PREP *Paper, pens or pencils*
Option 2 Identify famous voices.
MORE PREP *Recording of famous voices*

Starting Line

Option 1 Learn from a jackalope.
YOUNGER YOUTH *Disc 2 of* The Incredibles *DVD*

Option 2 Make a sheep pen.
OLDER YOUTH

Leading through the Session

Straight Away

Explore the Bible passage.
Bibles

The Turn

Discuss: Do you know the good shepherd?

Leading beyond the Session

Home Stretch

Option 1 Look forward to the coming week.
YOUNGER YOUTH *Chalkboard or dry erase board; paper and pens or pencils (optional)*
Option 2 Make it your own.
OLDER YOUTH *Reproducible 1, pens or pencils*

Finish Line

Option 1 Commit to help one another all week.
LITTLE PREP *Reproducible 2, pens or pencils*
Option 2 Swap contact information.
MORE PREP *Information cards, pens or pencils, time and equipment to communicate*

SESSION 1

WHOSE SHEEP ARE YOU?

Bible Passage
John 10:1–18

Key Verse
I am the good shepherd. The good shepherd lays down his life for the sheep.
—John 10:11

Main Thought
Christ has given all for us—we can trust him.

Bible Background

In this text we read another of the great "I am" statements that occur in John's Gospel. Once again in the midst of religious opponents Jesus employed a reference to familiar aspects of his culture to construct a figure of speech. Unfortunately the figure was lost on the Pharisees who were questioning him, so Jesus told them straight out, "*I am* the good shepherd" (10:11, emphasis added). It is tempting to isolate this verse from the surrounding context and treat it as a promise of Christ's tender protection. There is an old gospel song, "The Ninety and Nine" that dramatically portrays Jesus' parable from Luke 15 about a shepherd who refuses to accept the loss of even 1 percent of his flock and so risks life and limb to rescue a single lost sheep. There is joy at the shepherd's successful return, "for the Lord brings back his own." We are quite familiar with this line of interpretation. Sheep are among the dullest of God's creatures and thus are at great risk without the care and protection of a watchful shepherd, which of course Jesus is. However, faithful Bible reading requires us to pay attention to the context of this famous verse. If we do so, we will discover other important teaching points.

Jesus described himself as the good shepherd in the middle of another controversy with the Pharisees. It seems that the setting was Jerusalem in winter, very near the time of the Feast of Dedication (see 10:22). This was the Jewish religious celebration of Hanukkah, the festival of light. In his discussion with a group of Pharisees Jesus drew an extended metaphor based on something familiar to virtually everyone in the crowd—sheep and their care. It is probably unwise to try to make this into an allegory where Jesus is the good shepherd, Pharisees are thieves and robbers, and God is the gatekeeper. Rather, it was the identity of the good shepherd that was at issue here. True, the character, actions, and relationship of the good shepherd to his sheep were described and contrasted with the behavior of malicious intruders.

As an exercise on Christ's pastoral care, the passage made little sense to the Pharisees; as verse 6 states, "they did not understand what he was telling them." So Jesus laid aside the figurative language and in the plainest speech identified himself as the good shepherd.

In 10:16 Jesus declared that he has "other sheep that are not of this sheep pen." Although denominational competitiveness has diminished since the late twentieth century, Christians can still be tempted to play the game of insider-outsider. We do want to be the sheep of his flock, but we must also resist the temptation to believe that there are not others in other flocks who also recognize the shepherd's voice and heed his call. In the world of first-century Judaism "other flocks" would have meant the Gentiles, and the suggestion that they could also be Yahweh's people scandalized most self-respecting Jews. In the religiously tolerant world of the twenty-first century "other flocks" has been read to mean various Christian denominations, although their "otherness" is not as jarring as the Jew-Gentile distinction of the ancient world. Some people have interpreted verses such as 10:16 to mean that well-intended non-Christians who have never heard the gospel but endeavor to live morally upright lives in effect hear, however faintly, the Shepherd's voice and are saved. The point here is not to argue the merits of this latter interpretation. Rather, it is to illustrate a principle that seems to be at work in this text: Jesus is the good shepherd, and knowing him—recognizing his voice—does not come through affiliation with one specific group.

OPTION 1 (LITTLE PREP)

Discuss the importance of listening.

Divide students into small groups; distribute paper and pens or pencils to the groups. Ask the students in each group to think of situations where listening carefully is extremely important. For example, soldiers on the battlefront must listen carefully to instructions or risk losing their lives. Crime scene investigators sometimes have to listen carefully to audio recordings in order to pick out clues that are critical to solving a case. Ask the group members to write down their ideas. After a few minutes, bring the groups back together and invite group members to share their ideas with the rest of the class. Point out that God gave us two ears and only one mouth; this should give us some perspective on the importance of listening in a conversation!

Say, **The better you listen, the better communicator you will be.**

Warm Up

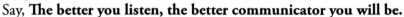

OPTION 2 (MORE PREP)

Identify famous voices.

Assemble a collection of famous voices and then play them to see if your students can recognize them.

Ask, **What makes us able to identify certain voices?** When we spend a lot of time listening to a person's voice, we are better able to identify that voice. We also get used to voices in certain contexts (for example, hearing a teacher's voice at school and a parent's voice at home). Hearing those voices in other places can sometimes make them more difficult to identify.

Say, **We all have certain voices that we know better than others.**

OPTION 1 (YOUNGER YOUTH)

Learn from a jackalope.

Show the cartoon short titled "Boundin'," on disc 2 of *The Incredibles* DVD set (likely also available online via a Google search). The clip is a little under five minutes. Afterward, discuss the following questions:

Starting Line

- **How did the sheep initially respond to being shaven?** The sheep's whole outlook on life had been dependent on his wool coat; without it, he was sad and depressed.
- **How was the jackalope able to help the sheep?** The jackalope taught the sheep that he still had many things in life to be glad about.
- **What does a shepherd do or provide for the sheep?** The shepherd is the caretaker of the sheep, providing food, water, protection, medical care, and sometimes shearing (cutting off the wool).

Say, **Let's see how Jesus acts as a shepherd for our lives.**

137

OPTION 2 (OLDER YOUTH)

Make a sheep pen.

Invite your students to build a sheep pen with whatever objects or pieces of furniture are around—desks, chairs, and so forth. The pen should have only one entrance. Ask your students to all stand inside the sheep pen. Ask, **What is the purpose of a sheep pen?** By corralling the sheep together in one secure location, they can be better protected from predators such as bears, lions, or wolves; they can also keep warm together, and the shepherd can make sure that no sheep wander off.

With your students still standing inside the "sheep pen," ask, **What do you think a shepherd would use as a gate for the sheep pen?** Allow students to respond; then, lie down in front of the opening. Explain that many times, when the sheep were in the pen for the night, the shepherd would lie across the opening of the sheep pen, acting as a gate to protect the sheep and prevent them from straying. Point out that this is a part of your responsibility as a "shepherd" in the youth ministry of your church—to care for, protect, and defend the students whom God has placed in your care. If there is time, give each student an opportunity to take the place of the gate. Talk about thoughts and feelings associated with being responsible for others.

When you are ready to move on, say, **Let's see how Jesus acts as a shepherd for our lives.**

Explore the Bible passage.

Explain that in Bible times, the title *shepherd* was sometimes used to refer to the leaders or caretakers of God's people. God himself was called the shepherd of Israel (see Psalm 23:1 and Isaiah 40:10–11), and God gave great responsibility to the leaders (shepherds) of Israel—a responsibility that they failed at time and time again. Jesus faithfully lived out his role as shepherd of God's flock. One time, on the Sabbath, he healed a man who had been born blind. This upset the Jewish leaders because they saw this as working on the Sabbath—which was against Jewish law. Jesus ended up in a discussion with some of the religious leaders; today's Bible passage is a part of what he said.

Straight Away

Read together John 10:1–18. Discuss the following questions:

- **Jesus began by saying, "I tell you the truth" (alternately translated as, "Verily, verily" or "I assure you"). Why did Jesus start this way? Did he lie at other times?** Jesus used this phrase to indicate the importance of what he was about to say—"Listen! Pay attention! Don't miss this!" Since Jesus is the Son of God, when Jesus speaks it is important that we listen.
- **What contrast did Jesus use in verses 1–4?** Jesus contrasted the sneaky behavior of "sheep stealers" to that of the honest shepherd. Point out that this illustration should still make sense to us, even if we don't own any sheep. The owner of a house has a key to the house and enters by the door; if we see someone climbing in the window of the house, then we can probably assume that person to be a thief. Entering by the gate demonstrates authenticity and truth.
- **Describe the relationship between the shepherd and the sheep.** The sheep listen to the shepherd because they know the shepherd. The shepherd knows each of the sheep by name. The shepherd leads the sheep, going ahead of them, and the sheep follow the shepherd because they trust the shepherd. If the shepherd calls your name, you know that you can trust the shepherd to lead you in safety.
- **Why did Jesus call himself "the gate" for the sheep?** If you used STARTING LINE, Option 2, reflect back on this activity. Ancient cities were walled for protection, and they had a limited number of gates. You didn't get in just any way—you had to enter by the gate. Jesus was again contrasting himself with those who did not truly care for God's flock. Jesus was saying that he is the way for us to enter into all that God has to offer.
- **What did Jesus promise for those who enter through the gate (Jesus)?** Jesus promised that they would be saved. Invite your students to define what they think this salvation is. Jesus also promised freedom (they will "come in and go out"), pasture (everything we need to sustain us in life), and life "to the full" (an abundant, overflowing life, far beyond our hopes and dreams).
- **Jesus went on to call himself the "good shepherd." What sorts of things does the good shepherd do?** The description now goes beyond the good shepherd providing good things for his sheep. The good shepherd actually gives his own life up for the sake of the sheep. This is contrasted with the hired hand, who runs away at the first sign of danger. The good shepherd also brings in the other sheep that are his. Emphasize that the adjective *good* can mean not only positive or kind but also effective (for example, a good soccer player

Note:

You can access *Strong's Concordance* (a helpful tool for finding the meanings of words in the Bible in their original language) at http://www.tgm. org/bible.htm.

Always be sure to check out thoroughly the content and links of any website before recommending that site to your students.

knows the requirements of the sport and does them well).

- **Whom was Jesus talking about when he mentioned these "other" sheep that he would bring in?** Invite students to respond. Some Jewish traditions taught that the Jewish people were the only ones in right relationship with God. But God's plan had always been to offer life to people anywhere who were willing to receive it (see Acts 13:47). This was a new stream of thought for most Jews—and those of us who are not Jewish should be thankful that God chose to include us "other sheep."
- **What did Jesus mean about taking his life up again after he had laid it down, and that no one could make him lay down his life?** Jesus beat death; he proved this by rising again on the third day after his crucifixion. Jesus went to his death voluntarily, on our behalf, even though he had multitudes of angels at his defense (see Matthew 26:53).

Say, **Jesus Christ, the good shepherd, gave all for his sheep—even his own life.**

The Turn

Discuss: Do you know the good shepherd?

Say, **Okay, this is a nice picture of the good shepherd—knowing the sheep personally, providing pasture and protection for the sheep, even laying down his life for the sheep. But is it possible or real to think we can experience these things *now*? Why or why not?** Invite students to respond. Different class members will be at different stages in their relationship with Christ. Some may be particularly skeptical at this time due to the actions and attitudes of professed Christians or even the perceived failure of Jesus to live up to his promises. Emphasize that this is what it's all about—a loving and patient shepherd who can handle the situations of his sheep. Just because a sheep is upset or having issues does not mean that the shepherd turns his back on the sheep. Remind your students that Jesus sticks by his sheep. Matthew 18:12–14 emphasizes Jesus' care and concern over even a single lost sheep. Be willing to share about times in your own life when you were not listening to the shepherd and about ways the shepherd brought you back into the fold.

When you are ready to move on, say, **Jesus Christ, the good shepherd, gave his life for you, that you might have an abundant life.**

Leading beyond the Session

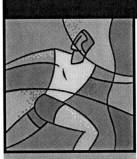

Home Stretch

OPTION 1 (YOUNGER YOUTH)

Look forward to the coming week.

Ask, **How is the voice of God usually portrayed in the movies or on television?** As a deep, booming voice—speaking in English. Now ask, **How is *Jesus* usually portrayed in the movies or on television?** He is often shown as tall, of strong build, and handsome, with long hair and a beard, sporting "anglo" features and speaking English. Point out that the beard and long hair were typical for Jewish men in Jesus' time, but beyond that we don't know what he looked like.

In fact, the Bible says in Isaiah 53:2 that he was basically "average" in his looks. And explain that Jesus could do all things, but he probably spoke Aramaic while he was here on earth.

Say, **As the good shepherd, Jesus calls each of us, by name, every day. How can we learn to recognize his voice?** You can either keep the group together to discuss this question as you write their answers on board, or break into small groups and give groups paper and pens or pencils with which to record their responses. Encourage all students to share their thoughts and ideas. Point out that we can know the voice of Christ when we know the heart of Christ—a heart that loves us, is concerned about every situation of our lives, and wants us to grow in our relationship with the Father. Jesus will not tell us to do things that are contrary to this.

Emphasize again that we are better able to identify a person's voice when we spend more time with that person—and this is true when we spend more time with Christ. Ask, **What are some real ways you could spend time with Christ this week?** Write students' ideas on the board. Encourage class members to think of things that a young person could realistically do—for example, reading a chapter of the Bible each day, not reading a whole book of the Bible each day.

Say, **If you pick just one of these ideas and carry it out this week, you can grow in your relationship with the good shepherd.**

. . . .

OPTION 2 (OLDER YOUTH)

Make it your own.

Distribute to students copies of "What Does Listening Really Look Like?" (Reproducible 1), or show it as a projection. You can either keep the group together to discuss these questions, or break into small groups for students to discuss. Possible responses are as follows:

- **How can you recognize Jesus' voice?** Point out that we can know the voice of Christ when we know the heart of Christ—a heart that loves us, is concerned about every situation of our lives, and wants us to grow in our relationship with the Father. Jesus will not tell us to do things that are contrary to this. Also, emphasize again that we are better able to identify a person's voice when we spend more time with that person—and this is true when we spend more time with Christ.
- **How does Jesus call your name?** Most of us do not hear the audible voice of Christ. However, through the Holy Spirit's presence within us, and through the kind words and actions of God's people, we can hear and know that Christ loves us.
- **How can Jesus bring freedom to your life?** Life in Christ means that we can be free from the grip of sin, free from the fear of death, and free from the worry of trying to fulfill a list of dos and don'ts in order to please God.
- **How can Jesus bring safety and security to your life?** God does intervene for our physical protection (see Psalm 121); he is also the guardian of our souls (see 1 Peter 1:8–9). In the perfect love of Christ, we need not fear the judgment of God (see 1 John 4:18).

- **How can you experience life more abundantly in Christ?** Christ has more than enough to meet the needs of all of God's children. Encourage class members to think of practical ways that they might enjoy the fullness of all that God has to offer.

Say, **The good shepherd calls to you, offering freedom, peace, and blessings for your life.**

Finish Line

Note:

As the group leader, enter into the agreements of some or all of the groups, so that students can see you model faithfulness and commitment to this kind of relationship.

Note:

Don't forget to distribute copies of the Portable Sanctuary to students before they go.

OPTION 1 (LITTLE PREP)
Commit to help one another all week.

Distribute to students copies of "Action Plan" (Reproducible 2). Break the class into small groups—if possible, by commonalities such as same schools, same geographic areas, and so forth. Ask each of the groups to come up with a plan of action for the coming week to help one another experience more abundantly the life that Christ has to offer. For example, maybe they can meet at the end of the week to review the Portable Sanctuary together, read independently a certain Bible passage and then get together to discuss it, or commit to phone or e-mail each other throughout the week. The focus of the action plans should be on reminding and encouraging one another to listen for the voice of the good shepherd calling their names.

Close the session in prayer, thanking God for the abundance he provides and asking God to help you be instruments of grace and peace in the lives of others.

OPTION 2 (MORE PREP)
Swap contact information.

Provide information cards for your students to fill out so that they can keep in contact with one another and support one another throughout the week. These cards should ask for the following information:

- Name
- Address
- City/State/Zip
- Phone number
- E-mail address
- Birth date
- School you attend
- Year you will graduate high school
- Name(s) of parent(s)
- Is it okay to share your info with the rest of the youth group?

A copy of an information card is provided on the Digital BRIDGES CD for you to print out and use. If you have already compiled this information, share it with the rest of the group (subject to students' permission). If not, you may need to take time later to put together the information you have just received and mail it or e-mail it to your students.

Together with your class, come up with a plan of action for reminding and encouraging one another to listen for the voice of the good shepherd in the coming week. For example, maybe you can set up an e-mail group through which you can send devotionals or encouraging messages to all your students, or perhaps you can design a "phone chain" where you call a certain person, that person calls the next person on the list, and so forth. Be sure to set a time limit in the evenings after which students should not call. If you place yourself at the beginning and end of the chain, you will be able to see whether students are following through with the action plan.

> *Note:*
>
> Don't forget to distribute copies of the Portable Sanctuary to students before they go.

143

What Does Listening Really Look Like?

Hearing is usually easy. If our ears are working, we hear noises all day—music, cars, wind, people's voices, and so forth. But *listening—hearing, understanding,* and *responding—*takes effort.

There is a story about two men who were walking in downtown New York. One said, "Did you hear that bird?" The other man replied, "How can you hear anything above the noise of the streets, people, and construction?" The first man said, "We hear what we are tuned in to hear." He then proceeded to yell loudly—no one noticed. But then he took out a handful of change and threw it onto the sidewalk. Immediately, heads turned and people stopped to pick up the money.

What are *you* tuned in to hearing? Be intentional about what—and whom—you listen to.

• How can you recognize Jesus' voice? _____
_____

• How does Jesus call your name? _____
_____

• How can Jesus bring freedom to your life? _____
_____

• How can Jesus bring safety and security to your life? _____
_____

• How can you experience life more abundantly in Christ? _____
_____

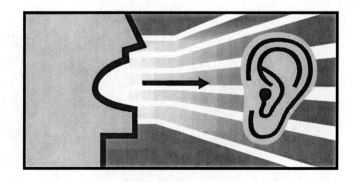

Action Plan

There is nothing worse than being moved to respond and then doing nothing about it. *Here is your chance to not do nothing.*

In your group, come up with a plan of action for the coming week to help one another experience more abundantly the life that Christ has to offer. What can your group members do to remind and encourage one another to listen for the voice of the good shepherd this week? How often will you do this?

_____

_____

_____

_____

Here are the people I am going to connect with this week:

Name	E-mail	Cell
_____	_____	_____
_____	_____	_____
_____	_____	_____
_____	_____	_____
_____	_____	_____
_____	_____	_____
_____	_____	_____
_____	_____	_____
_____	_____	_____

Portable Sanctuary

Day 1

Lost and Found

Have you ever been lost? I spent four hours in the lost and found area at an amusement park once. I hated being there, knowing that all the time my family and friends were off riding rides and eating food. I set out to find my parents. When I found them they were having a great time and were happy to see me. They never even knew I was lost—they just thought I was off with friends going on a few rides.

Sometimes we feel lost and wonder if God is really there. It seems we can't find God. We feel alone, abandoned, and afraid.

Questions and Suggestions

- Read Ezekiel 34:11–16. Write out all of the "I will" statements of God from this passage. What kind of picture does this paint of God in your mind? Why? How have you experienced God in this way?
- Read the passage again. What is it about the care of God that you are thankful for? Pray about it.

Day 2

The Lord Is My Shepherd

Have you ever been hit and it took you by surprise? I recently read a story about a meteor the size of Rhode Island hurtling through space toward earth. Had it hit us, we would have been wiped out. I am thankful God put the planet Jupiter where he did. Jupiter's size and location provide Earth perfect protection from meteors. Only small pieces of meteors are able to escape Jupiter's powerful gravitational pull—and by then they are so destroyed that we see these remnants as just "shooting stars" in the night sky.

Questions and Suggestions

- Read Psalm 23. Write or draw the picture that this brings to your mind. (For example: I see a beautiful, refreshing pool of water surrounded by lush trees. I feel a warm breeze blowing. I see God smiling as we sit at the table and eat together.)
- Consider your own life—your past, your present, and your future. Look for God. Do you see God? Where? How? Pray about it.

Day 3
The Lost Sheep

I have three kids. One hot August day, we went to the beach. The crowd was amazing—everywhere you looked, there were large groups of people. Suddenly, we realized one of our sons was not around. As time stood still and my conversation with God went into fast forward, I searched and searched. Then as quickly as my son had disappeared, I found him. He looked panicked, and I am sure I looked worried. As I hugged him, I felt an overwhelming sense of peace and thankfulness. I think God feels the same every time we come to him.

Questions and Suggestions

- Read Matthew 18:10–14. Have you ever lost something and then found it? How did you feel?
- What do you think it means to be a "lost sheep"? How does God go and look for the ones who have wandered off? Why is one person so important to God? Pray about it.

Day 4
Jesus the Example

"Our behavior will not be changed long with self-discipline, but fall in love and a human will accomplish what he never thought possible. The laziest of men will swim the English channel to win his woman. I think what Rick [pastor of a church] said is worth repeating that by accepting God's love for us, we fall in love with Him, and only then do we have the fuel we need to obey." —Donald Miller, *Blue Like Jazz: Nonreligious Thoughts on Christian Spirituality* (Nashville, Tenn, Thomas Nelson Publishers, 2003), 86.

Jesus was going all over the place meeting needs. He was moved by compassion—so many sheep who needed a shepherd! He compared them to a large harvest that didn't have enough people to bring it in. So he challenged us to step out, to be workers who help with the harvest.

Questions and Suggestions

- Read Matthew 9:35–38. Now, read Donald Miller's quote again and respond. What would it mean for you to be moved with love and compassion for others?
- Pray that God will send workers—including you—into the harvest of life.

Day 5
A Psalm for Giving Thanks

I live in a home. I drive a car. I eat food when I am hungry. I have clothes. I pay my bills. I buy fun stuff. My family and I are taken care of. We meet freely and regularly with other followers of Christ (this is called the church), and we can have events centered on God without anyone telling us to stop. I can study my Bible in the local coffee shop. I can pray for my food at a restaurant. I am a sheep who enjoys the provision, the peace, and the abundance of good pasture—and I am thankful.

Questions and Suggestions

- Read Psalm 100. What do you shout for? Why? How is God providing "pasture" in your life?
- Look again at verse 5. Create something (with words, paint, pencil, clay, or so forth) that is a response to God's enduring, unfailing love.
- Write out some real ways for you to daily live out "thanksgiving" and "praise." Pray about it.

Leading into the Session

Warm Up

Option 1 Share some beliefs.
LITTLE PREP

Option 2 Read some obituaries.
MORE PREP *Obituaries from a newspaper*

Starting Line

Option 1 Find out what you can do.
YOUNGER YOUTH *Reproducible 1*

Option 2 Discuss your world.
OLDER YOUTH *Chalkboard or dry erase board*

Leading through the Session

Straight Away

Explore the Bible passage.
Bibles

The Turn

See Christ here and now.
Bibles, chair

Leading beyond the Session

Home Stretch

Option 1 Read a resurrection story.
YOUNGER YOUTH *Reproducible 2*

Option 2 Discuss a video clip.
OLDER YOUTH *The Matrix DVD*

Finish Line

Option 1 Comfort others with Jesus' words.
LITTLE PREP *Bibles, paper, pens or pencils*

Option 2 Envision Lazarus's coming alive.
MORE PREP *Trip to a local cemetery*

SESSION 2

JESUS CONQUERS DEATH

Bible Passage
John 11:1–44

Key Verse
Jesus said to her, "I am the resurrection and the life. Those who believe in me, even though they die, will live, and everyone who lives and believes in me will never die."
—John 11:25–26 (NRSV)

Main Thought
Jesus' power extends even over death.

149

Bible Background

Death and life pervade this familiar passage from John. Lazarus, Jesus' friend and the brother of Mary and Martha, had been ill, so gravely ill that the sisters had sent word asking Jesus to come to their aid. Mary and Martha did not refer to Lazarus by name in their message—they simply stated, "Lord, the one you love is sick." The sisters had pinned their hope on Jesus' healing power, but Lazarus died before the Lord arrived. Grief ran so deep that Jesus himself wept with Lazarus's mourners.

Jesus was not in the region of Judea when he received word of Lazarus's illness. A return to Judea and the town of Bethany—a suburb of Jerusalem—was a dangerous journey for Jesus. Jerusalem was the center of Jewish religious leadership and thus the home of many people who were bent on his destruction. Indeed, the disciple Thomas considered the trip to Judea so dangerous that he said to his fellow disciples, "Let us also go, that we may die with him" (11:16). This trip was a matter of life or death for Lazarus, and it was also a life or death matter for Jesus.

Novelist and children's book author Madeleine L'Engle believes that even Christians speak euphemistically of death. We use phrases such as "passed on" or "stepped from this life into the next" because we prefer not to say "died." Death carries such an awful finality that even people of faith can scarcely confront it. Of course, it is also true that Christian faith means that death is not final. But until we cross over we will never again see or speak to those who have died, and death is final in that sense.

It is this finality of their brother's death that Mary and Martha could not escape, not even after Jesus arrived. They believed in the general resurrection of the dead and that Lazarus would rise on that day. But until that day they assumed, quite naturally, that nothing could be done. When Jesus asked to see the tomb, Martha's sense of propriety took over and she warned him that the body would already have begun decomposing. Nevertheless, Jesus insisted and told her, "I am the resurrection and the life." Now the sisters and the curious onlookers came to insight, for Jesus beckoned to Lazarus and the dead man walked out of his grave.

The Gospel of John uses a distinctive word, *semeion,* for miracles such as the raising of Lazarus. This word is best translated as "sign." In John's Gospel miracles are not so much explosions of the power of the Kingdom as they are signs that Jesus was indeed who he claimed to be. Very often, as in this text, the miracle or sign is associated with a direct statement such as "I am the resurrection and the life." The sign points out the reality of that claim. It was not a mere assertion but was borne out by events such as the raising of Lazarus.

Of course Lazarus was raised from the dead only to die again. Not many of us can say that we will taste death twice as Lazarus did—but we will all come to that end. It has been said of life, "None of us will get out of this alive." Even so, death does not have the last word. That word belongs instead to Jesus, who reveals the Father—the one who transforms defeat into victory. God is the power for life, not death, for all who believe in Christ.

OPTION 1 (LITTLE PREP)

Share some beliefs.

Warm Up

Ask your students, **What are some things you believe?** Do not provide any clarification beyond this, but simply repeat the question. Invite a variety of answers—coffee is good, the sky is blue, fire is hot, water is wet, if I bang my head against the wall it will hurt, the Bible is God's Word, and so forth. Now ask, **Where did those beliefs come from? Why do you believe them?** We believe many things because people have taught them to us, because we have observed them to be true, or both; in our spiritual lives, we believe some things simply because the Bible states them to be true or because of God's Spirit working in us (this is a part of *faith*).

Say, **Here are some ways that people have expressed their faith, and the things that happened to them** (these are also available as a projection on the Digital BRIDGES CD):

- **"Are you the king of the Jews?" asked Pilate. "Yes, it is as you say," Jesus replied.—Jesus Christ, crucified outside Jerusalem almost 2,000 years ago.**
- **"For to me, to live is Christ and to die is gain."—Paul the Apostle, beheaded in Rome for his faith, 65 AD.**
- **"We shall not end our lives in the fire, but make a change for a better life."—Julius Palmer, burned at the stake in England for his faith, 1556.**
- **"This is the end for me, the beginning of life." Dietrich Bonhoeffer, hung in Germany for his faith, 1945.**
- **"Yes, I believe in God." Cassie Bernall, shot to death for her faith, 1999.**

Invite your students to reflect on the things they just said they believe. Ask, **What beliefs would you be willing to die for? Why?** Point out that in the case of each of the quotes you just shared, there were other people who were not willing to die for their faith.

When you are ready to move on, say, **Some of our beliefs are more important than others.**

. . . .

OPTION 2 (MORE PREP)

Read some obituaries.

Bring to class the obituary section from your local newspaper. You may wish to make copies of the page or to bring newspapers from different days. Many newspapers have websites where their obituaries are also posted. Invite your students to read some of the different obituaries. Who is the youngest person mentioned? The oldest? Can your students tell, from the obituaries, what kinds of lives these people lived? What would your students like to have mentioned in their own obituaries? Ask, **Do you know what the purpose of an obituary is?** An obituary is published so that we can be informed of a person's death, know when and where the funeral service will be, and know about the life of the deceased person.

Note:

Be sensitive to any students who have recently lost friends or loved ones.

When you are ready to move on, say, **Each of us will have his or her own obituary someday—because each of us will die someday.**

Starting Line

OPTION 1 (YOUNGER YOUTH)

Find out what you can do.

Distribute to students copies of "The Power of the Mind" (Reproducible 1), or show it as a projection. See if anyone can decipher what this cryptic message says. Here is the correct translation:

Can you read this? Only 55 percent of people can. If you can read this, you have a powerful mind. I couldn't believe that I could actually understand what I was reading. According to research at Cambridge University, it doesn't matter in what order the letters in a word are; the only important thing is that the first and last letter be in the right places. The rest can be a total mess and you can still read it without a problem. This is because the human mind does not read every letter by itself, but the word as a whole. Amazing, huh? I always thought spelling was important!

Chances are, some students will be able to read this message. This is because the mind "straightens out the mess" in the middle of the words, using the beginning and ending letters and the context as a guide. Ask, **Do any of you have some other amazing powers or talents?** Invite students to respond and to show the rest of the class what they can do.

Say, **Let's take a look at one of the powers Jesus had—the power to raise people from the dead.**

OPTION 2 (OLDER YOUTH)

Discuss your world.

Ask, **What are the prevalent beliefs we see around us each day—things that others believe are important and true and would like for us to believe in too?** Invite students to consider the beliefs that are promoted by their peers, their parents, and the media. Friends sometimes want us to value having fun, even when that fun is illegal or goes against our personal convictions. Parents often want us to value hard work and a good education. The media wants us to value good looks, wealth, and entertainment as the marks of a successful and happy life. Write students' responses on the board. Now ask, **Which of these influences is strongest in your life? Why?** Invite students to respond.

Say, **Let's look at the beliefs of Mary and Martha, some friends of Jesus.**

Explore the Bible passage.

This story is somewhat lengthy but it is powerful. Proceed with your study by considering the text in three sections.

First, read together John 11:1–16. Discuss the following questions:

Straight Away

- **What sort of relationship did Jesus have with Mary, Martha, and Lazarus? How can you tell?** This family was obviously very close to Jesus. Mary later anointed Jesus' feet with expensive perfume and then dried them with her hair (see John 12:1–11). The message the sisters sent to Jesus simply said, "The one you love is sick," yet Jesus knew the person they were talking about. The text points out that Jesus loved Martha and her siblings (verse 5). The disciples knew that Bethany was a dangerous place for Jesus to return to, so Jesus' determination to go was further evidence of his love for this family.

- **What was odd about Jesus' reaction when he heard that Lazarus was sick?** He stayed where he was two more days before heading to see Lazarus. Remind your students of the common mode of transportation at that time—walking. It would take a while to get to Bethany, yet Jesus delayed going. Point out that Jesus knew that God would be glorified through the miracle he would do in Lazarus's life, and in verse 11 he indicated that he knew Lazarus would be dead when he got there, although the disciples didn't understand what he meant.

Now, read together John 11:17–37. Discuss the following questions:

- **How much hope was there for Lazarus's recovery?** Lazarus had already been dead for four days. Explain that Jews believed the soul hung out by the body for three days after death in hopes of returning to it, but irrevocably departed on day four. In the minds of most of the people, all hope was gone at this point. Martha told Jesus that she knew he could have prevented Lazarus from dying—and she indicated that she knew it was not too late for Jesus to help (see verses 21–22).

- **Jesus told Martha that Lazarus would rise again. What did Martha think he meant, and how did Jesus respond to her?** Martha thought that Jesus was referring to "the resurrection at the last day" (the end of time). Jesus responded by affirming that there would be such a resurrection; he said that we can experience such a resurrection through belief in him, and he confirmed Martha's belief in this fact.

- **What does it mean to believe in Jesus in this way?** Invite students to respond. The word used here means to have faith, to trust in something, to be fully convinced that it is true, to acknowledge it, to rely on it. This is a personal trust that produces action, submitting ourselves to God and positively confessing that Jesus Christ is Savior and Lord (master, controller, authority) of our lives.

- **Verse 35 is the shortest one in the entire Bible. Why would Jesus weep if he knew that he was going to bring Lazarus back to life?** Invite students to respond. Jesus was moved by Mary's sorrow and by the sorrow of the other people who were there. Emphasize that Jesus cares intimately about our lives and about the things that concern us. To think about the Son of God weeping when we weep is a powerful thing.

Now, read together John 11:38–44. Discuss the following questions:

- **What objection did Martha have to Jesus here?** She didn't want the stone removed from the entrance of the tomb, fearing that the smell of the decaying body would be terrible. If any of your students have ever gotten a good whiff of rotting food, they will have at least a small idea of why Martha objected. From Jesus' response (v 40), we see that Martha still did not understand what Jesus was about to do.
- **What did Jesus state again as the purpose of the miracle he was about to do?** It was so that the people would believe that God had sent him.

Say, **Jesus loved others and he wanted them to believe in him for eternal life.**

The Turn

See Christ here and now.

Ask, **What verses from this story do we often hear quoted, preached, or taught about?** Verse 35 ("Jesus wept") is mentioned due to its brevity and its indication of Jesus' heart for us. Verses 25 and 26 are extremely important for followers of Christ. Jesus stated plainly who he is, what he does, and how we can experience the blessings of his work.

Take a good chair and place it in front of the group. Ask, **How many of you believe that this chair will support you without collapsing to the floor?** Assure your students that this is not a trick question; you can prove this by sitting in the chair yourself. Now ask, **What is the only way you can really prove to me that you believe this chair will support you?** Students can do this only by actually coming forward and sitting in the chair. Point out that believing in a chair and acting on that belief by sitting in the chair is wonderful—but it will not save anyone.

Say, **Believing in Jesus Christ for eternal life—and then acting on that belief—will save you.**

Note:

This would be a natural time to extend an invitation for students to place their faith in Jesus Christ. See "Leading a Teenager to Christ" in the back of this book for some tips.

OPTION 1 (YOUNGER YOUTH)

Read a resurrection story.

Distribute to students copies of "Resurrection Story" (Reproducible 2), or show it as a projection. After reading the piece, discuss the following questions:

Home Stretch

- **Do you believe this story? Why or why not?**
- **Have you seen people on television or elsewhere who seem to have the gift of divine healing? Do you believe what these people do? Why or why not?**
- **Is there a limit to the kinds of healing or miracles God can do? Are there certain limits God seems to choose to follow? Explain.** God can do anything; the Bible contains many stories of resurrections, healings, and miracles that defied the laws of nature. But there are certain kinds of healings that seem not to occur. For example, people do not grow back arms or legs that they have lost; people who are burned continue to have scars; and people who have been dead for long periods of time do not come back to life.
- **Jesus said that his followers would do even greater miracles than he had done, that he would do anything as long as they asked in his name (John 14:11–14). Why aren't there more instances of people being raised from the dead today?** Some have proposed that the days of miraculous healings are past; some have proposed that our lack of faith prevents us from participating in miracles; some have proposed that only certain people have the gift of divine healing; and some believe that our sin and rejection of God as a nation prevent miracles. Be honest with your students as you wrestle with this issue.

When you are ready to move on, say, **Jesus promised to do great things through us—and we should be willing to be used for his glory.**

OPTION 2 (OLDER YOUTH)

Discuss a video clip.

Show your students a clip from the movie *The Matrix*. If any students are not familiar with this movie, use the following synopsis:

Thomas Anderson was living an ordinary life in what he thought was the year 1999, until he learned that it was really 200 years later. He finds out that the world has been taken over by computers that have created a false version of twentieth-century life—the "Matrix." The computers are drawing power from human beings while using the Matrix to keep the human slaves satisfied. Anderson, pursued constantly by "Agents" (computers that take on human form), is hailed as the one who will lead the human beings to overthrow the machines and reclaim the earth.

In the scene you will show, Anderson—also known as "Neo"—is using a simulator to be trained to fight back in the Matrix. Start the video at 48:15 (the beginning of Scene 15, "Morpheus/Neo Matchup"). Stop the video at about 52:06, after Morpheus says, "Do you think that is air you are breathing?" Be sure to stop the video at this point, due to some language that is used later in the scene.

Note:

There is no objectionable content in this scene; however, be sure to preview any other scenes before showing them to your students.

155

After showing the clip, discuss the following questions:

- **Why did Neo think that he kept getting beaten by Morpheus?** He thought that Morpheus was too fast.
- **What was Neo's real limitation?** Neo's limitation was in what he believed. Morpheus pointed out that, in reality, he (Morpheus) had no greater strength or speed than Neo did.
- **How was Neo's experience like Martha's experience with Jesus?** Martha was in distress because her brother had died. However, Jesus told her that if she believed in him, her brother would live. Point out that God's promises to us are great and God's power is unlimited; we experience defeat or distress when we fail to believe this.

Say, **Jesus promised to do great things through us and for us—if we will only believe.**

Finish Line

OPTION 1 (LITTLE PREP)

Comfort others with Jesus' words.

Provide paper and pens or pencils to your students and spend some time writing notes of encouragement and comfort to persons you know who have recently lost loved ones. There may be persons in your congregation who are grieving, or students may have family or friends who are grieving. Here are some possible verses to include:

- Psalm 121:1–2
- John 11:25–26
- 2 Corinthians 1:3–4

Talk with your students about appropriate words of comfort for the bereaved. For example, it may be true that God can bring something good out of the situation—but that might not be too comforting at the present time to someone who has experienced an unexpected loss. Saying, "Your loved one is with Jesus" would not be appropriate if someone feels that the deceased person had rejected God. It is often best to say, "I'm sorry for your loss. My thoughts and prayers are with you," or something similar.

Close the session by praying together for those who have suffered loss and by thanking God for the promise of eternal life. You could provide stamped envelopes and ask students to address and mail their notes, but you will increase the certainty of their delivery if you collect them and mail them yourself.

Note:

Don't forget to distribute copies of the Portable Sanctuary to students before they go.

OPTION 2 (MORE PREP)

Envision Lazarus's coming alive.

Make arrangements to take a trip to a local cemetery. (Be sure you have the permission of your pastor or youth pastor and the proper permission and forms to take students off-site.) The idea is not to be spooky but instead to help students envision the resurrection of Lazarus. If possible, go to an above-ground vault, as this will be more similar to Lazarus's tomb.

Ask students to close their eyes as you summarize the events of John 11:1—44 using words similar to the following:

Jesus loved Lazarus. And Lazarus was dead—dead and buried. Lazarus had already been in the grave for *four days*. The grass was already growing again, and the tombstone was up. Family and friends were still around, crying and hurting. Jesus was hurting for them. He told them to open up the grave. What a strange idea—but they did it. Jesus prayed: "Father, thank you for hearing me!" Then he shouted, "Lazarus, come out!" And right there, in front of everybody, Lazarus climbed out of the grave, still dressed in the suit they had buried him in.

Invite your students to open their eyes and look around. Emphasize that we will each end up in a place like this someday—but that's not the end of the story. One day the graves will open, and those who have placed their faith in Christ will rise to eternal life. Say, **Can you imagine what this place will be like on resurrection day—all these graves opening up? It won't be scary—it will be a time of celebration!**

Close the session by praying together for those who have suffered loss and for any needs in your group, and by thanking God for the promise of eternal life.

> *Note:*
>
> If you have any students who have recently lost friends or loved ones, you may wish to use Option 1 instead.

> *Note:*
>
> Don't forget to distribute copies of the Portable Sanctuary to students before they go.

The Power of the Mind

Can you raed tihs? Olny 55 pnerect of plepoe can. If you can raed tihs, you hvae a preowufl mnid.

I cdnuol't blveiee taht I cluod aulaclty uesdnatnrd waht I was rdanieg. Aocdcrnig to rsreecah at Cmaribgde Uinervtisy, it dseno't mtaetr in waht oerdr the ltteres in a wrod are; the olny iproamtnt tihng is taht the frsit and lsat ltteer be in the rghit pcleas. The rset can be a taotl mses and you can siltl raed it whotuit a pboerlm. Tihs is bcuseae the huamn mnid deos not raed ervey lteter by istlef, but the wrod as a wlohe. Azanmig, huh? I awlyas tghuhot slipnelg was ipmotrnat!

Resurrection Story*

Enoch E. Byrum was a minister, evangelist, author, and Christian leader at the end of the nineteenth century. People were often miraculously healed in response to Byrum's prayers.

One time Byrum was called to go and pray for a woman named Nancy King, who was very sick. Byrum said, "As I entered the house, a strange feeling came over me ... as if I had been ushered into the presence of death." Byrum continued: "In a few minutes she breathed her last, and her spirit departed." But he was convinced that God wanted to glorify his name by raising the woman from the dead.

Byrum and the other people present continued to pray; some of the others also believed that this woman would be raised up in answer to prayer. They all prayed aloud, going forward and laying their hands on the woman. In the name of Jesus they rebuked the power of death and asked the Lord to restore her to life again. Suddenly the woman sat up in bed, brushed her hair back, and said, "Why did you call me back? I would have been in glory." The woman told of being carried upward to heaven, where the beauty and the angelic singing were indescribable. After a time, two angels carried her back to earth, where she could see her body lying in the bed. The next thing she knew, she was sitting up.

It is estimated that Nancy King was dead several hours before God raised her to life again.

* See E. E. Byrum, *Miracles and Healing* (Anderson, Ind: Gospel Trumpet Company, 1919), 254–260.

Portable Sanctuary

Questions and Suggestions

- Look again at John 11:38–44. What a huge risk to take—rolling the stone away. Why do you think the people were willing to risk? Was the risk worth it?
- Look at your own life. What risks are you taking? What risks *should* you be taking? What are you willing to risk for Jesus?
- There are hundreds of thousands of churches in North America. How many of them sit empty most of the time? What risks should we take to change the emptiness?

N O T E S

Day 1
Listen!

Listen. What do you hear around you? Is it something that can change you? People sometimes say very profound things—and some even live out their beliefs.

"Gandhi believed Jesus when he said to turn the other cheek. Gandhi brought down the British Empire, deeply injured the caste system, and changed the world. Mother Teresa believed Jesus when He said everybody was priceless, even the ugly ones, the smelly ones, and Mother Teresa changed the world by showing them that a human being can be selfless." —Donald Miller, *Blue Like Jazz: Nonreligious Thoughts on Christian Spirituality* (Nashville, Tenn, Thomas Nelson Publishers, 2003), 106.

Questions and Suggestions
- Read John 11:25–27. Do your beliefs shape you in such a way that you can change the world? What about changing the life of someone you know?
- What you believe is not what you say you believe—what you believe is what you do. Does your life reflect your belief in the Resurrection and the Life, Jesus Christ? Pray about it.

Day 2
The Effects of Belief

Being seven years old is a great time. Everything is still fun—even school, with lots of snacks and recess. When I was seven I was curious about everything, so riding in the back of my grandparents' huge car with all its knobs and handles was *amazing*. There was one button that would always pop back up about twenty seconds after I pushed it down. My grandparents saw what I was doing and warned me not to touch the lighter—I could get burned. But I didn't believe them. Excitedly, I pushed it down; it popped up and I pulled it out. There was this bright red, glowing area that I decided to touch. I can honestly say that I have never touched a car cigarette lighter ever since.

Questions and Suggestions

• Read John 11:38–44. What happens when we say we believe? How does that impact our lives? Where and when does Jesus show up?
• Would you like to see the glory of God in your life? Pray about it.

Day 3
Time to Listen

Today was crazy: up at 5:30 AM for a three-hour meeting, then to the office, then to take my kids to music, baseball, and—you get the idea. Life can get pretty full. Just when I think I can't handle any more, something else important comes along and I feel the need to add it to my schedule. I have to be very intentional to listen for the voice of God in my day—and to listen to what my wife and kids are trying to say. It is important for me to take time to really listen.

Questions and Suggestions

• Read John 11:20. I don't know how Martha heard that Jesus was coming, but she responded. She left whatever it was she was doing and went out to meet Jesus.
• Write down the things that you are busy doing—all of them. How busy is your life?
• Jesus wants to hang out with you. How does that make you feel? Do you want to hang out with him? Pray about it.

Day 4
The Same Person?

Think back as far as you can. What do you remember? I remember falling asleep in church almost every Sunday when I was little. I also hated to swim. Then I started playing in a friend's spa and began to like being in the water. We moved to a house with a pool and once summer hit, we swam—all day long. We would swim so much we would get sick from swallowing too much pool water. Many years later, I still love being in the water.

Think back over the past five years of your life—ten years, if you can. Think back to when you started in the youth group. Do you recognize yourself? Are you the same person you were then? How have you changed? Why have you changed?

Questions and Suggestions

• Read John 11:1–44. What changes do you see? What changes happened because of Jesus?
• What changes have happened in *your* life because of Jesus? What do you want to have happen? Pray about it.

Day 5
Talking a Risk

When I started surfing I was terrible. The waves constantly beat me up and threw me all over the place. The very first time I went surfing I wasn't prepared. By the time we were done, I was numb, hurting, and planning on never surfing again. However, I gave it another try. What a risk that was! Twenty years later and I still surf! Now I am in better control of the board. I still get beat up sometimes, but I know how to use the power of the waves in my favor.

Leading into the Session

Warm Up

Option 1 Conduct a phone quiz.
LITTLE PREP *Candy or another small prize (optional)*

Option 2 Observe a big house.
MORE PREP *Pictures of a big house; or, trip to see one*

Starting Line

Option 1 Play hide and seek.
YOUNGER YOUTH

Option 2 Think about greater things.
OLDER YOUTH *Chalkboard or dry erase board*

Leading through the Session

Straight Away

Explore the Bible passage.
Bibles

The Turn

Find comfort in the way.

Leading beyond the Session

Home Stretch

Option 1 Chart out comfort and greater things.
YOUNGER YOUTH *Reproducible 1, pens or pencils*

Option 2 Find Barney in Acts.
OLDER YOUTH *Bible, Reproducible 2, pens or pencils*

Finish Line

Option 1 Ask in Jesus' name.
LITTLE PREP

Option 2 Act in Jesus' name.
MORE PREP

SESSION 3

JESUS IS THE WAY

Bible Passage
John 14:1–14

Key Verse
Jesus said to him, "I am the way and the truth and the life. No one comes to the Father except through me."
—John 14:6

Main Thought
Through Jesus we can know—and be with—God the Father.

The theme of reassurance plays a prominent role in John 14. In the face of what had just transpired in the upper room, Jesus' disciples were in deep need of his assurance. Jesus had performed the most menial of tasks when he washed the disciples' feet; this was no way for a rabbi to behave, and Jesus himself said that only later would the disciples understand this act. Already confused, the disciples then were thrown into dismay when Jesus announced that he was about to be betrayed and that Judas was the traitor. Matters could only have gotten worse when Jesus then said to Peter, "Before the rooster crows, you will disown me three times!" (13:38). Thus concludes chapter 13. Small wonder that Jesus immediately followed all of this by saying, "Do not let your hearts be troubled."

Jesus' teaching here is not easily mastered. Who has not lain awake through the night, unable to sleep because of a troubled heart? How can we secure our lives against all that threatens them and is beyond our control? The disciples felt threatened in the upper room, and so do we when we think about all the things that can go wrong. We jog, lower our cholesterol, and count calories only to hear the cardiologist say that genetic history is the biggest factor in heart disease. Job security threatens us or our children and we are anxious. In the face the disciples' turmoil and fears, Jesus asked them—and asks us—to trust him and God. It is the same thing to trust God as to trust Jesus.

Death hung heavy in the air. The disciples did not need to be prophets to figure out that Jesus' betrayal would lead to his death. "The Jews," as John called them, had been seeking Jesus' death for a long time. With a traitor in their very midst and the group gathered in Jerusalem there was little chance that Jesus would once again elude the religious authorities. For some time Thomas had been of the opinion that another trip to Jerusalem might mean death for all of the disciples. With the exception of John, all the disciples *would* suffer martyrdom, although not immediately.

Jesus did not promise his followers an escape from death. He did not tell the disciples not to worry because they were about to fly off to heaven. They would have to die. However, Jesus reassured them with a promise that might be labeled "the great nevertheless." On the other side of death is the place to which Jesus would soon go and where he had prepared places for his followers. He promised to return "and take you to be with me" (v 3). Then Jesus told the disciples that they already knew the way. Once again confusion reigned. Thomas and Philip were full of questions. They objected that they did not know the way and that they wanted him to show them the Father. It is not always easy to see through to the truth when fear and confusion threaten to overwhelm us. Jesus answered Thomas, "I am the way and the truth and the life." And to Philip's plea Jesus replied, "Anyone who has seen me has seen the Father."

There was a note of impatience in Jesus' reply to Philip, but after answering this backward student Jesus made a surprising promise. Those who have faith in him will do works even greater than his. But such power comes at a price. In order for such works of faith to happen Jesus had to go to the Father. Spiritual power would descend on the disciples, but at the cost of earthly fellowship with their Master. This did not mean, however, that they would be abandoned; a Comforter, the Holy Spirit who stands alongside, would come once Jesus had returned to the Father.

OPTION 1 (LITTLE PREP)

Conduct a phone quiz.

Quiz your students on their knowledge of telephones by asking the following questions:

- **Why does a telephone (not cordless) usually work even when the power is out?** Telephone companies use lead acid cells to supply their own DC power.
- **What is the length of ring and pause for a typical household phone?** Two seconds of ringing and four seconds of pause.
- **Who is typically credited with inventing the first telephone?** Alexander Graham Bell.
- **What were the old folding-style cellular phones designed after?** The communication devices in the Star Trek television series.
- **Why do most phone numbers in television shows or movies begin with 555?** This prefix is rarely used and never for private numbers. When real prefixes are used, people call them, and the people who really have those numbers get a flood of calls.

If you wish, you can award candy or another small prize to the student who gets the most correct answers.

Invite your students to share how much time they spend on the phone or texting in a typical day. Point out that it's important to listen closely when using a telephone, since we can't see the person we're talking with. In a text or e-mail, it can be difficult to determine the mood or attitude of the other person.

Say, **Sometimes we misunderstand what someone is trying to tell us.**

Note:

For more interesting phone facts, go to http://en.wikipedia.org/wiki/Telephone.

. . . .

OPTION 2 (MORE PREP)

Observe a big house.

Take your students on a quick tour of a large house that is close to where you meet. (Perhaps someone in your congregation has such a home, or perhaps you know a realtor who can give you a tour of such a house.) Try to pick the biggest house possible—one that would have room for all of your students to live—and then some! If you cannot make such a visit, bring some pictures of a huge house.

Debrief your experience by discussing the following questions:

- **Would you like to live in a house like this someday?**
- **What kinds of things would you like to have in your "dream house"?**
- **How much do you think a house like this might cost?**

Explain that a house becomes a home when we live in it. This might have been just a nice house to us, but to the people who live there, it's home.

Say, **A good home can provide a lot of security to our lives.**

Note:

Be sure you have the proper permission to take your students off-site.

Starting Line

OPTION 1 (YOUNGER YOUTH)

Play hide and seek.

Tell your students that you will be playing a special round of hide and seek, where one person hides and everyone else tries to find that person. Pick one eager volunteer and send him or her out to hide; however, make sure you and the remaining students watch where this person goes. If your volunteer does not see you watching, the group will find him or her very quickly. If the volunteer does notice that you are all watching, he or she will protest that it is not fair. Carry on anyway, playing just one round of the game.

After everyone has returned to the room, ask, **How is this game *supposed* to work?** You are not supposed to see where the person goes to hide; the whole point is in the search. Point out that your find was easy because you knew exactly where the person was going.

Say, **Let's see how Jesus said we can get to where he was going.**

· ·

OPTION 2 (OLDER YOUTH)

Think about greater things.

Ask, **What are some outstanding accomplishments you are aware of—sports records? Who are the best athletes and teams, and what is so great about them?** Invite students to respond. Write on the board the names and records they mention. Following are some suggestions you might use:

- **Jerry Rice holds the record for most career touchdowns—208.**
- **Ty Cobb holds the record for the highest career batting average—.366.**
- **Florence Griffith-Joyner holds the record for the women's 100 meter dash—10.49 seconds.**

Discuss the following questions:

- **How many of you think you could beat one of these records?**
- **What would it take to beat one of these records?** A person would need incredible speed and athletic ability—and probably a long career—in order to beat one of these records.
- **What would you say if I promised you that you could beat one of these records?** This would be an amazing promise—almost unbelievable.

Say, **Let's see how Jesus promised us that we could do some great things.**

Note:

This list of athletes and records is available as a projection on the Digital BRIDGES CD.

Explore the Bible passage.

Explain that Jesus and his disciples were hanging out together celebrating the Feast of Passover. This was a feast of hope and life celebrating deliverance and new beginnings, something that Christ would soon take to a new level for his disciples—and for us. Jesus had washed their feet and told them to love one another as he had loved them. He said that he would be leaving and they could not follow him—yet. This was a lot for the disciples to process. Jesus then gave some words of comfort—and some incredible promises—to his friends.

Straight Away

Read together John 14:1–14. Discuss the following questions:

- **What did Jesus promise about his Father's house—the place he was going?** He said that it has plenty of rooms, that he was going to prepare it for his friends, and that he would not fail to come back for his friends. Invite your students to talk about what sort of preparations Jesus might be doing in heaven to get it ready for his people.

- **Jesus' statement in verse 6 ("I am the way and the truth and the life") is an often-quoted verse. What do you think it means?** Invite students to respond. The disciples did not understand that Jesus was going back to the Father. Jesus clarified himself by saying that he is the way to the Father, the revealer of the reality (truth) about the Father, and the bringer of eternal life.

- **What does it mean to say, "If you know me, you know my Father"?** This indicates the closest of relationships. Point out that we all bear some of the characteristics of our birth parents—height, body build, skin tone, eye color, personality, likes and dislikes, natural talents, and so forth. Our personalities and likes and dislikes are also formed by the people we spend time with—family and friends. We might look at a person and get some sort of idea about what that person's parents are like. But Jesus and the Father are so close that when we have seen Jesus, we have seen the Father—so close that they are one.

- **Philip and the disciples were still struggling to have faith in who Jesus was. What two things did Jesus give as reasons that they should believe in him?** First of all, they had spent "a long time" together (v 9); probably about three years. As disciples of a rabbi, this was not some 8-to-5 job; they traveled together, ate together, and stayed together 24/7. Jesus then said that they should at least believe in him based on the miracles they had seen him do. Flip back through the Gospel of John and review the awesome things that Jesus did. Jesus had proven that he had the power of God—and that he was completely trustworthy.

- **What are some ways that we *know* and *see* and *experience* Christ today?** Invite students to respond.

- **Jesus finished off with some amazing promises. What are they, and how do you respond to them?** Jesus said that those with faith in him would do what he had been doing—and even greater things. He also promised to do anything that his followers ask in his name. Encourage your students to express their reactions to these promises.

- **What was the key to these greater things happening?** Jesus was going to be with the Father. Point out that it would be nice to have Jesus here with us in the flesh. The disciples would certainly have anticipated the loss of Jesus' leaving. But Jesus is now with the Father—at the top of it all, working so that we can do the greater things he promised.

- **Did these promises come true for the disciples?** Absolutely. The Book of Acts is full of stories of Peter, Philip, Paul, and others; they performed healings, cast out demons, raised the dead, and shared the word and the love of God in the same way as Jesus had.

Say, **Through Jesus, the disciples knew God the Father.**

The Turn

Find comfort in the way.

Point out that in the New International Version of the Bible, John 14:1–4 is subtitled, "Jesus Comforts His Disciples." Ask, **What would have been so comforting to the disciples about what Jesus said?** Jesus basically said that he was going home, to the Father, but that there was room for his friends to come along, too, and that he would come back for them. Invite your students to think about a beloved father leaving on a trip to purchase a new home, the best home ever. The kids would be waiting in anticipation, every day, for the father to return and take them to the new home. Ask, **What if the father just called and said, "Okay, the new house is ready. Come on over!"?** The kids would not know where the house was—and would have no way to get there even if they did. Jesus promised to be the way to the Father and to life—and to be the life itself. Now ask, **What if the father left no food or money while he was gone preparing the house?** The kids would starve to death or be evicted before he returned. But Jesus promised that while he is gone, we will do the same things he did while he was here.

Say, **Jesus has provided for our needs while he prepares a place for us—and he will be back for us.**

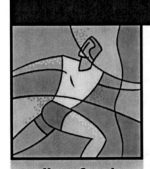

Home Stretch

OPTION 1 (YOUNGER YOUTH)
Chart out comfort and greater things.

Distribute to students copies of "Comfort and Greater Things" (Reproducible 1), go over the instructions, and allow time for students to complete the assignment. Afterwards, invite those who are willing to share what they wrote. Be open in sharing your own needs for comfort from God, the ways you express your trust in God, and the greater things you would like to see God do in your life. Point out that the things Jesus did were all for God's glory and the benefit of others. The purpose of God's doing greater things in and through us is not for fun or fame—it's to help others and point them to God.

When you are ready to move on, say, **God is ready to step into the situations of your life, providing comfort and doing great things.**

OPTION 2 (OLDER YOUTH)

Find Barney in Acts.

Distribute to students copies of "I Love You, You Love Me" (Reproducible 2), or show it as a projection. Students can complete the handout alone or in small groups, or you can work on it all together. If students work alone or in groups, allow time for them to write down their thoughts; then bring everyone back together. Invite those who are willing to share what they wrote.

Read again to your students Jesus' words in John 14:6—"No one comes to the Father except through me." Ask, **If you were trying to share Christ with a person who did not know Christ, how might that person respond to these words?** Be honest about the exclusivity of this passage, while acknowledging the fact that Jesus ministered to people and loved them into the kingdom of God; he did not beat them up or shame them into believing in him.

When you are ready to move on, say, **To live as Jesus lived means to love as Jesus loved.**

OPTION 1 (LITTLE PREP)

Ask in Jesus' name.

Say, **Jesus said we could ask for anything in his name, and he would do it. So, Where's my new car? Where's my million dollars? I asked for God to heal my sick friend and he didn't do it. What's the deal?** Allow students to respond. Explain that this is not just a "blank check" promise—and there's more to asking for something "in Jesus' name" than just saying the words "in Jesus' name." To ask in the name of Jesus also means:

Finish Line

- **to ask in his authority.** This passage says that we do have the authority to do the things that Jesus did.
- **to ask with his heart.** Asking for the fulfillment of our selfish wish list is not asking with the heart of Jesus. Asking for God's blessings and best for others is asking with the heart of Jesus.
- **to ask in his will.** There are times when things that seem good to us do not seem to be God's will. Even though we may not always understand God's will, Jesus asks us to trust him (John 14:9–10).

Close the session in prayer. Give your students some silent moments to ask for better understanding of God's power, God's heart, and God's will. Finish your prayer time by asking for God's power and peace to be unleashed in your students' lives, in Jesus' name.

> *Note:*
>
> Don't forget to distribute copies of the Portable Sanctuary to students before they go.

> *Note:*
>
> WARM UP, Option 2, of next week's session calls for students to each bring a piece of fruit. Ask them to do this if you intend to use this option.

OPTION 2 (MORE PREP)

Act in Jesus' name.

Explain that there's more to Jesus' promise to do anything we ask in his name than just saying "in Jesus' name" at the end of our prayers. To ask in the name of Jesus also means:

- **to ask in his authority.** John 14 says that we do have the authority to do the things that Jesus did.
- **to ask with his heart.** Asking for the fulfillment of our selfish wish list is not asking with the heart of Jesus. Asking for God's blessings and best for others is asking with the heart of Jesus.
- **to ask in his will.** There are times when things that seem good to us do not seem to be God's will. Even though we may not always understand God's will, Jesus asks us to trust him (John 14:9–10).

Ask, **With all you have walked through and experienced in this session, what will you do differently this week? What can we do right now, today, to help each other and to act in Jesus' name?** Invite students to respond. Doing something now does not have to be a complicated affair. Your students might take responsibility to clean and straighten up the room you have just used, to thank the host of the home you met in, to open the door and greet people in worship, to straighten the pews and pick up trash after worship, or something similar. Emphasize the fact that doing the things Jesus did does not always mean walking on water or healing people who are blind—we can all do as Jesus did by loving and serving others every day.

Close the session in prayer. Give your students some silent moments to ask for better understanding of God's power, God's heart, and God's will. Finish your prayer time by asking for God's power and peace to be unleashed in your students' lives, in Jesus' name.

Note:

Don't forget to distribute copies of the Portable Sanctuary to students before they go.

Note:

WARM UP, Option 2, of next week's session calls for students to each bring a piece of fruit. Ask them to do this if you intend to use this option.

Comfort and Greater Things

Rewrite the verses below in your own words.

John 14:1–4

[1]"Do not let your hearts be troubled. Trust in God; trust also in me. [2]In my Father's house are many rooms;

_____

if it were not so, I would have told you. I am going there to prepare a place for you.

_____

[3]And if I go and prepare a place for you, I will come back and take you to be with me that you

_____

also may be where I am. [4]You know the way to the place where I am going."

_____

John 14:6–7

[6]Jesus answered, "I am the way and the truth and the life. No one comes to the Father except through me.

_____

[7]If you really knew me, you would know my Father as well. From now on, you do

_____

know him and have seen him."

_____

John 14:10–14

[10]Don't you believe that I am in the Father, and that the Father is in me? The words I say to you are not just

_____

my own. Rather, it is the Father, living in me, who is doing his work. [11]Believe me

_____

when I say that I am in the Father and the Father is in me; or at least believe on the evidence of

_____

the miracles themselves. [12]I tell you the truth, anyone who has faith in me will do what I have

_____

been doing. He will do even greater things than these, because I am going to the Father. [13]And I

_____

will do whatever you ask in my name, so that the Son may bring glory to the Father. [14]You may

_____

ask me for anything in my name, and I will do it.

_____

How could these verses bring comfort to you? _____

_____

Every time you get in a car, you trust that it won't fall apart while you're riding down the road. How do you
show trust in *God?* _____

_____

What are some *greater things* (v 12) you would like to see happen in your life? Why? _____

_____

I Love You, You Love Me

I love you, you love me....——Barney, the purple dinosaur

John Buchanan once said, "People who think and write about church growth perhaps should pay a little more attention to the book of Acts. The earliest Christians simply acted like Christians, like friends and followers of Jesus. They devoted themselves to love and compassion. It doesn't say they devoted themselves to church growth or evangelism. It says they devoted themselves to caring for one another and for others, and the world was compelled by their authenticity, the integrity of the life they lived in the world. Their life together was the very best evangelism."*

What do you think of this quote? _____
_____

In today's world, Christianity isn't loved by everyone. Some people label Christians as hypocrites. Others find our claims and our behavior to be oppressive and arrogant. Some just feel that the things we claim about God and Jesus Christ are not true, or don't apply to them. But Jesus said that he is the way and the truth and the life. How does this claim fit with people of other cultures and other faith traditions? _____
_____
_____

How can we model the love and compassion of Christ in our neighborhoods? at our schools? in our homes? at our work? where we hang out? _____
_____
_____

* From "Give Me That Old Time Religion," sermon preached at Fourth Presbyterian Church in Chicago, April 25, 1999, as found at http://fourthchurch.org/sermons/1999/042599.html..

Portable Sanctuary

Questions and Suggestions

- Go back and read over all of this week's Portable Sanctuary—especially the stuff you wrote down. What stands out to you? Why? Are there some things in your life that will change because of what you discovered this week? What are they?

- Of what you wrote down, what do you most want to remember? Pray about it.

NOTES

Day 1

Remember

One hundred watt, single phase. If you know what that means, I congratulate you. I know now, but I didn't know then. I was helping a friend put in an electric circuit breaker—100 watt, single phase—so we could host a large concert. I was curious about this equipment (here's the stupid part) and, using my middle and pointer fingers, reached my hand out to touch two of the pipes coming into the breaker box. In what felt and sounded like slow-motion, my friend yelled for me to stop, while my two fingers acted as a conduit for electricity to run up my arm, down my back, and through my feet.

My friend, the electrician, was laughing as I staggered back, trying to catch my breath. He said, *"Never touch those!"* I never have since—and I never will again.

Questions and Suggestions

- Read John 14:1–14. Write out your answers: What do you remember from your experiences with Jesus? What *should* you remember? Why? How will you remember better?

- Pray that you will daily be aware of the power and peace of God in your life.

Day 2

Peace Out, Napoleon

Remember Napoleon Dynamite? His older brother, Kip, was pretty funny. Remember the change in him after his girlfriend came to town? She began to really transform him. At one point, Kip said to Napoleon,

"Peace out." Comparing Kip near the end of the movie to how he was at the beginning, we see a huge change.

The phrase "peace out" is nothing new, but the power of peace is much larger than a statement or phrase. Jesus tells us not to be troubled: *be at peace.*

Questions and Suggestions

• Read John 14:25–31. Our peace is based on our belief in Christ. We know he is trustworthy and that he gives us a foundation of peace we can build on.

• What does Christ's peace, given to us, look like for you today? How will you be intentional in building on the peace of Christ? How can you share your peace with others? Pray about it.

Day 3
Keep Your Head Up

Yosemite National Forest is truly amazing. I spent eleven days hiking through it in college. The third day was brutal. We were headed to a waterfall to camp for the night. It was a long way and we had to go up many hills and mountains. We kept reminding each other not to look down, but rather to look around, to enjoy the journey, and to remember the destination. We pushed on and finally made it.

Jesus has promised to prepare an incredible place for us—a place where we will get to hang out with him for eternity. Many places in the Bible refer to this as a huge party. Sounds amazing, doesn't it?

Questions and Suggestions

• Read Isaiah 65:17–25. What do you envision as you read this description of the new heavens and new earth? How does it feel knowing you have a place prepared for you in eternity?

• An eternal party in heaven. How does that look for you? How could that impact your life *today?* Pray about it. Plan to enjoy the party.

Day 4
There You Are

My daughter is a toddler and she likes to dance, so we have enrolled her in a tap and ballet class. Every time I drop her off for class, I look her in the eye and tell her I will be back to pick her up. One week, I was on the other side of the room when she came out, and she didn't see me. She stood still, a serious look on her face as she scanned the room. When she finally saw me, she got this huge smile and laughed confidently while she skipped to me, hugged me, and said, "There you are!"

Jesus promised to return and take us with him. Think of Jesus looking you in the eye and saying, "I'm coming back for you so we can be together in my Father's house forever."

Questions and Suggestions

• Read Acts 1:1–11. What did the angels say to those looking up?

• Jesus will come back some day, coming down from heaven in the same way as he went up to heaven. Are you ready for that day? Pray about it.

Day 5
I Remember Now!

Novelist James Baldwin said, "I really do believe that we can all become better than we are. I know we can. But the price is enormous—and people are not yet willing to pay it."[1] Are you ready to move forward with God? What do you think the price might be for you? Titus 1:16 says that some people "claim to know God, but by their actions they deny him." What do your actions say? You may have studied the Bible and been to church for years now. What do you remember? What do you remember from just this past week?

1. From http://www.pbs.org/wnet/americanmasters/database/baldwin_j_interview.html.

Leading into the Session

Warm Up

Option 1
LITTLE PREP
Walk and talk.

Option 2
MORE PREP
Play the fruit basket game.
A piece of fruit for each student, paper bags

Starting Line

Option 1
YOUNGER YOUTH
Complete a survey.
Reproducible 1, pens or pencils

Option 2
OLDER YOUTH
Conduct a horticulture lesson.
Chalkboard or dry erase board (optional)

Leading through the Session

Straight Away

Explore the Bible passage.
Bibles

The Turn

Talk about remaining in the vine.
Reproducible 2, pens or pencils

Leading beyond the Session

Home Stretch

Option 1
YOUNGER YOUTH
Discuss fruit bearing.
Chalkboard or dry erase board

Option 2
OLDER YOUTH
Discuss pruning.
Pruning shears; branches (preferably live) to prune (optional)

Finish Line

Option 1
LITTLE PREP
Make a plan of action and pray.

Option 2
MORE PREP
Cultivate and evaluate.
Small vine shoots; Internet access (optional)

SESSION 4

CONNECTED TO THE VINE

Bible Passage
John 15:1–17

Key Verse
As the Father has loved me, so have I loved you. Now remain in my love.
—John 15:9

Main Thought
If we stay connected to Christ, we can love as Christ loved.

Bible Background

In a previous session of this book we considered the significance that ancient thinkers attached to the idea of friendship (see Bible Background for "Imitating Christ"). It is now time to explore that idea more completely since in John 15 Jesus elevated his followers to the status of friends.

The ancient philosopher Aristotle thought that friendship could be expressed in any of three forms. He did not think that these three were in any way equal and did not offer what we might think of as a theory of love or friendship. Rather, true to his method of inquiry, Aristotle studied the phenomenon of friendship as he found it among human beings. On this basis he ranked the forms of friendship into three categories. The lowest form of friendship is a relationship we develop because of what the friend can do for us. In these "friendships of utility" the "love" we have for the friend is badly tarnished with our own self-interest. One wonders whether this can even qualify as a form of love and friendship, except that we do know of such relationships. Higher in Aristotle's ranking are what he called "pleasure friendships," relationships in which we simply take delight in the company of our friend. The highest degree of friendship is based in virtue. Here people become friends on the basis of the mutual regard they share and their esteem for the other. Characteristic of these relationships is each friend's desire to do good to each other for, as Aristotle said in words that anticipated the Bible, "It is better to do good than receive it." The word that expresses love in such friendships is translated into English as benevolence. But Aristotle had a problem here, because benevolence suggests that one friend occupies a higher station than the other. Benevolence flows from the stronger partner to the friend.

Aristotle died more than three centuries before the birth of Jesus, whose saying on friendship in John 15 elevated the discussion beyond anything we find in pagan philosophy. Here Jesus told his disciples that they would no longer be servants. The master-disciple relationship was dissolved so that from then on his followers would be known as "friends." Unlike Aristotle's virtue friendship, when Jesus declared his followers to be friends he placed them on equal footing: "Everything that I learned from my Father I have made known to you" (15:15). But how can this be? Surely we dare not say that we know what Jesus knows. True enough, but Jesus did not say that. He said that he taught the disciples everything that he learned from the Father. Any teacher knows that there are often discrepancies between what was taught and what appears to have been learned.

That Jesus raised his followers to the status of friendship is grounds for both celebration and caution. One theologian has noted that Jesus made "friend" a Messianic title to be added to "prophet, priest, and king." Jesus is the friend of sinners who makes it possible for them to enter into friendship with God. He teaches a way of life that, if followed, can be described as preparation for eternal friendship with God. That's good news and reason to celebrate. What then is the caution? In the nineteenth century Protestants became enamored of the idea of Jesus as friend. This notion was captured by gospel songs and hymns of the era such as "What a Friend We Have in Jesus" and "In the Garden." While it is wholly appropriate to sing of Jesus our friend—after all, that's the title he gives his followers—in the hands of some twentieth-century writers the intimacy of friendship threatens to degenerate into something approaching disrespect. Even the most intimate of friendships are characterized by the respect of one friend for the other. How much more do we need to respect the friend who is also the Lord of the universe?

OPTION 1 (LITTLE PREP)

Walk and talk.

This activity will provide an "icebreaker" for your students, as well as help them begin to think about the topic of today's Bible study.

Either pair students up or put small groups together. Ask the pairs or groups to start at point *A* (somewhere you designate) and walk to point *B* (a route that will take a few minutes to complete). As students are walking, they should discuss these questions in their pairs or groups:

- **What's the longest-term friendship you have ever had? What made (or makes) the friendship last?**
- **Why is it important to share our lives with each other?**
- **If you could be any fruit in the world, which fruit would you be and why?**

Return to your meeting space after your walk is complete. Say, **Like an apple tree or a grapevine, God has designed us to grow in our relationships.**

Warm Up

Note:

These questions are available on the Digital BRIDGES CD for you to print out.

• •

OPTION 2 (MORE PREP)

Play the fruit basket game.

Ahead of time, ask each student to bring one piece of fruit to class. Encourage creativity—the larger or more obscure the fruit, the better! Students should keep the fruit hidden in something such as a paper bag. Provide extra fruit and bags for visitors or forgetful students.

Invite everyone to sit in a circle, holding their bags of fruit. There should be no empty chairs. Ask one student to stand in the middle of the circle, holding his or her bag of fruit (this person's chair should be removed). That person should yell out a word or phrase that describes the fruit, without saying the name of the fruit. For example, if the fruit is a banana, the student could say "Yellow," or "Grows on a tree," or "Grows in a bunch." All other students with fruit that fits that description must get up and exchange chairs. The person in the middle should also try to sit in one of the empty chairs before someone else does. The person left standing is now *it*.

Repeat the process several times, trying to keep the action moving quickly. Eventually, guide students to call out things such as "Edible" or "Has seeds," which will get everyone up and about at the same time. After several rounds, let students take turns guessing what type of fruit is in each person's bag. A person who guesses correctly gets the other person's fruit. Those who guess wrong should give their fruit to the person they guessed about. The person with the most fruit at the end is the winner (they get to keep the fruit).

Say, **Just as God caused this fruit to grow, God has designed us to grow in our relationships.**

Starting Line

OPTION 1 (YOUNGER YOUTH)

Complete a survey.

Distribute to students copies of "Fruit Survey" (Reproducible 1), or show it as a projection. Students can complete the activity alone, in pairs or groups, or all together. Ask them to be honest in their responses. If you divide the class into pairs or groups, bring everyone back together after a few minutes and invite those who are willing to share their responses with the rest of the group. Encourage your students to keep their eyes open for the fruit of God's Spirit in their lives even if they don't see that fruit yet, and to seek to cultivate aspects of God's fruit through prayer and God's Word. Point out that fruit will grow only when it is well-watered and connected to the tree or vine.

When you are ready to move on, say, **Let's see what Jesus had to say about growing in him.**

. . . .

OPTION 2 (OLDER YOUTH)

Conduct a horticulture lesson.

Ask, **Does anyone know what *horticulture* is?** Depending on your locale, some of your students may know that this means the growing of plants, including fruits and vegetables. Now ask, **Does anyone know the five areas of study included in horticulture?** Again, any of your students who live on farms or are involved in FFA may know some of these: *floriculture* (flowers), landscape *horticulture* (landscape plants), *olericulture* (vegetables), *pomology* (fruits), and *postharvest physiology* (maintaining quality and preventing spoilage of crops). By now you may have bored some of your students, but keep pressing on! Ask, **What kinds of college courses will you need to take if you want to major in horticulture?** Courses might include *biology, botany, entomology, chemistry, mathematics, genetics, physiology, statistics, computer science,* and *communications.*

When you are ready to move on, say, **Let's see what Jesus had to say about "spiritual horticulture"—growing in him.**

> *Note:*
>
> You may wish to use the chalkboard or dry erase board to assist with your horticulture lesson.

Leading through the Session

Straight Away

Explore the Bible passage.

Read together John 15:1–17. Discuss the following questions:

- **According to this passage, what are the two types of branches?** Those branches that bear fruit and those that do not.
- **What happens to those branches that don't bear any fruit?** The gardener (God) cuts those branches off; they wither and are picked up, thrown into the fire, and burned. Invite students to elaborate on what this might mean. The bottom line: separation from God is not a good thing!
- **So life is a piece of cake for those branches that do bear fruit, right?** Wrong; if we bear fruit then we can be expected to be pruned or trimmed clean. Again, invite your students to discuss what it might be like to be

"pruned by God." Pruning cuts the branch; it is a painful process that removes things from our lives. If we remain in God, then we can expect times of "pruning" when God will work in our circumstances now to produce something good later on. Refer to verse 3; if we have followed the words of Christ, then we have already experienced a part of the pruning process, leaving our old lives behind for God's way.

- **How do we know if a "branch"—a person—is hooked up to the vine?** That branch will be alive and bearing fruit. Encourage your students to think of the kinds of fruit that children of God should bear. Galatians 5:22–23 (mentioned in STARTING LINE, Option 1) lists several aspects of the fruit of the Spirit—qualities or characteristics that should be present in our lives if God's Spirit lives in us. It is also true that, just as an apple tree bears apples and a grape vine bears grapes, the life of a Christian should bear other Christians—people who see God in us and respond to the seed of God's love that we plant in them.

- **Jesus asked his disciples—and he asks us—to remain in his love. Why would anyone ever walk away from the love of God?** Invite students to respond. Many people commit to many things at first but then lose their motivation later on; this even happened with some of Jesus' followers (see John 6:66–69). Most of your students will have games, books, clothes, or other items that they were very fond of at first but then gradually these slipped into disuse. Some Christians get "burned" by betrayal or hypocrisy in the church, or they experience tragedy and feel that God has let them down.

- **So, how do we remain in Christ's love, and what are the results?** We remain in Christ's love by doing what he says (verse 10). This is a very simple statement—but very difficult to do for many people! Jesus said that as we do this, we will have his joy and that our joy will be complete (full, overflowing, lacking nothing). With this connection, Jesus said that we are no longer just his followers—we are his friends. Invite your students to imagine the joy and the power in being a friend of the Son of God and of God himself!

- **Jesus repeated a "command" in this passage—what is it?** Love each other as I have loved you (verse 12); love each other (verse 17). Invite students to define a "Jesus kind of love"—unselfish, unconditional, consistent, patient, eternal, serving, seeking the good of others. This is not dependent on circumstances or feelings.

- **This passage is rather long and it contains a lot of stuff! How would you summarize it?** Invite students to respond. One possible answer: Jesus is connected with God, and we should stay connected to him. Then God will work in our lives; it might hurt sometimes, but it will bring even greater things. Jesus' command is for us to love others as he has loved us. If we do this, we will bear fruit for God, experience great joy, and be counted as friends of Jesus Christ.

Say, **Jesus Christ, the true vine, invites us to be connected to his joy and power.**

The Turn

Note:

This handout is also available on the Digital BRIDGES CD as a projection.

Talk about remaining in the vine.

Point out to your students that when Jesus was talking to his disciples about vines and branches, he was approaching his last hours of freedom; he would soon be arrested and crucified. Although he would be raised to life again, he would be taken back to heaven soon after that. Jesus knew what was about to happen, and he wanted to encourage and strengthen the disciples to remain in him—even though he would soon be gone.

Distribute copies of "Remain in Me" (Reproducible 2) and invite students to complete the handout; you can have them do this alone, in small groups, or all together. After allowing time to complete the work, invite those who are willing to share what they wrote. Emphasize the following points:

- To remain in Jesus indicates to stay in relationship with him, to abide in him, to continue to dwell in him, to be present with him, to stand with him.
- Remaining in Jesus' love involves obeying Jesus' commands—doing what he asks us to do.
- If we do not recognize and understand how we can remain in Jesus, we become as a withered branch—destined to be discarded.

When you are ready to move on, say, **Jesus has shown us how to remain connected to God through him.**

Leading beyond the Session

Home Stretch

OPTION 1 (YOUNGER YOUTH)

Discuss fruit bearing.

Use the chalkboard or dry erase board to help give your students a visual summary of today's Bible passage. Draw a vine and ask, **Who is the true vine?** Jesus (label your vine). Now draw a man standing by the vine with pruning shears in his hand and ask, **Who is the gardener?** God (label your gardener). Now draw two branches on the vine (with no fruit on them yet) and ask, **Who are the branches?** You and I—*people* (label your branches). Point to one of the branches and ask, **What happens to the branches that don't grow anything?** They're cut off and burned (place a big *X* through this branch). Now draw fruit on the other branch and ask, **What happens to the branches that *do* bear fruit?** The gardener trims them clean so that they will produce even more fruit (erase the fruit from this branch and then draw even more fruit on it).

Invite students to consider where they stand in this diagram. Are they even branches yet, connected to the life of Christ? If so, are they producing fruit for God? Your purpose is not to make any students feel bad for their "fruit production" but to encourage them to build stronger connections to Jesus Christ, the true vine.

When you are ready to move on, say, **In Christ, you can draw a new picture today—one in which you are bearing much fruit for God.**

OPTION 2 (OLDER YOUTH)

Discuss pruning.

Bring to class a pair of pruning shears. Ask, **Do you think these could take off a finger?** Absolutely. (*Note:* Do not experiment with this idea!) Pruning shears are designed to use a little force on the operator's part to lop off big branches. Ask, **Have any of you used something like this before?** If possible, go outside and allow volunteers to take turns pruning some branches.

Help students to better understand the pruning process by discussing the following questions:

Note:

Make sure you have permission from your church gardener before cutting off any branches.

- **What does a tree look like when it's just been pruned?** Freshly pruned trees often look barren and ugly. Sometimes there are hardly any leaves left at all.
- **What happens in the spot where a branch was cut off?** The spot tends to sprout multiple branches. This can mean a thicker tree in the end—but these new branches need to be pruned and maintained so that the tree stays healthy.
- **How does pruning indicate the skill and the care of the one doing the pruning?** A gardener only prunes a tree that he or she cares about. And a skilled gardener knows just where and when to prune; the result is a bigger and stronger tree.
- **What sorts of things might God "prune" from our lives?** At times things seem to turn bad just when they were going well. We might lose a friendship, lose a good job, fail a test, or fail to make the team. However, this does not mean that God doesn't care. God often works through these times to bring greater opportunities and blessings into our lives—things we might never have experienced otherwise.
- **How can we see God's love in the "pruning times" of our lives?** God prunes the branches that he loves—those who are remaining in Christ the vine. If we are truly being pruned, then we know that God is working in our lives.

Say, **If you feel that you are being pruned today, be encouraged! God is working to make you strong and to bring fruit to your life.**

OPTION 1 (LITTLE PREP)

Make a plan of action and pray.

Ask each student to come up with a plan for the week to stay connected to Christ the vine and to produce fruit for the kingdom of God. Say, **Christ chose us to go and bear lasting fruit—and he promised to do what it takes to make that happen. Our responsibility is to remain connected to the vine and growing.** Invite students to call out simple, practical ideas for remaining in the vine this week. Perhaps they can commit to using the Portable Sanctuary each day, or to considering how they are showing Christ's love before they speak and act, or to e-mailing daily notes of encouragement to one another. Encourage the expression of any and all ideas—someone may suggest something that is just what another person needs to grow this week.

Finish Line

Close the session in prayer, asking for God's strength during times of pruning and seeking greater love and growth as you and your students remain in the true vine, Jesus Christ.

Note:

Don't forget to distribute copies of the Portable Sanctuary to students before they go.

• •

OPTION 2 (MORE PREP)
Cultivate and evaluate.

Provide for each student a small vine shoot to take home and plant. (Check with a local nursery; or, you can clip some ivy and let it sprout roots in water.) If you wish, put *I am the vine; you are the branches.—John 15:5* on the pots or containers that contain the vines. Encourage students to plant their vines in an appropriate location at home, or to grow them and tend them indoors for a while if it is winter.

Take some time with your students to evaluate their experience with this book during the past several weeks. Were the instructions in the book clear and user-friendly? Was the content challenging enough for your students? Were the activity options adequate for your class? Did you make use of the supplemental Digital BRIDGES CD? Survey your students, fill out the postage-paid form in the back of this book, and mail it in.

Close the session in prayer, asking for God's strength during times of pruning and seeking greater love and growth as you and your students remain in the true vine, Jesus Christ.

Fruit Survey

If you have ever lived in a different town or attended a different school, do you think people are nicer in your current town and in your current school? Explain. _____

_____

_____

Do you think people were nicer a year ago than they are today? How about ten years ago? How about one hundred years ago? How about in Jesus' time? Explain. _____

_____

_____

Galatians 5:22–23 says, "But the fruit of the Spirit is love, joy, peace, patience, kindness, goodness, faithfulness, gentleness and self-control." If you could have only one of these qualities for your life, which one would you choose? Why? _____

_____

Which one of these qualities would you say that you are *strongest* at? Why? _____

_____

Which one of these qualities would you say that you are *weakest* at? Why? _____

_____

What is the key to producing good, healthy fruit? _____

_____

Remain in Me

What do you think it means to "remain in Jesus"? _____

_____

What do you expect to happen in your life as a result of Jesus' presence in your life? _____

_____

How are you taking action to make sure that you are remaining in Jesus?

_____

_____

Are you experiencing "complete" joy in your life? What might that look like? _____

_____

Contrast what it looks like to remain in Jesus and what it looks like when we are not remaining in him:

Remaining in Jesus	Not Remaining in Jesus
_____	_____
_____	_____
_____	_____
_____	_____
_____	_____
_____	_____

Why is it important to recognize and understand how we can remain in Jesus? _____

_____

Portable Sanctuary

Day 1
Being Clean

Do some hard work today—of any sort. Play a sport, clean the garage, mow the lawn, or run a mile. How does your body feel? Are you tired and dirty? Now take a shower—wash yourself clean. Savor the contrast between the dirty you and the clean you. After you get cleaned up, read Ephesians 5:25–27. Christ has cleansed you from every sin, every stain, every blemish, every dirty mark. He washes you through his word (see John 15:3) and through his Spirit. He sees you as holy and blameless—radiant.

Questions and Suggestions

- Can you think of things you have done that have left a bad mark on your life? Picture them as dirty stains on your body. Confess them to Christ and watch them disappear as you realize he has cleansed you from them. You are clean, forgiven, beautiful. How do you feel?
- You may make mistakes sometimes, but Christ is always ready to cleanse, forgive, and restore you. Honesty and confession will keep you clean. Don't take that for granted. Tell Jesus about how you feel. Pray about it.

Day 2
Dirt

When we're talking about being clean, dirt might seem to be a bad thing—but this is not always so. Go get some dirt. Pick up a handful and feel its texture. Let it sift through your fingers. Dirt is filled with the nutrients to nurture life and bring growth. What is there in your life that is like good dirt—making you strong, giving you deep roots, causing you to grow? Who are the people helping you to grow? What are you doing to grow? God wants you to grow. God wants to help you grow. He wants to bring new life into your life.

Questions and Suggestions

- Read Matthew 13:1–9, 18–23. What kind of dirt are you planted in? What good things are growing in you? What is growing spiritually? Are weeds trying to choke out your love for God? How will you uproot them?

- Grab another handful of dirt. Hold it tight. How can you grow to be more like Christ? Everything you need is in him. Let him shape (prune) you and you will be amazed at what grows in your life. Pray about it.

Day 3
Roots

Go to a faucet and turn the water on. Watch it run. Put your hand in it and feel it wash over your fingers. Watch the water go down the drain, unused. Now, fill a cup with water and find a plant. Water the plant, watching the water soak down into the dirt. Think about how water helps plants grow. Trees and plants flourish by a stream because they are close to their source of life—water. You, too, can flourish in your life when you are close to your source of life—God.

Questions and Suggestions

- Read Jeremiah 17:7–8. Imagine yourself as a tree. God can nourish you with love, just as water nourishes a tree. Are you planted near God's stream of love? Are your roots tapped into that stream? Do you trust God completely?

- What do you need to soak up more water in your relationship with God? How can you move closer to God's stream of love, mercy, and life? Pray about it.

Day 4
Photosynthesis

Find a plant or tree that is bearing fruit. If it is wintertime, you may need to go online or to a nursery to do this. Look closely at what is produced by the plant. Notice the colors, textures, smells, shapes, and sizes. Does the plant look healthy? Does it look strong? How much light is shining on the plant? Through a process called photosynthesis, plants convert light into the energy they need to grow and survive.

Questions and Suggestions

- Read Galatians 5:22–23. Think about "spiritual photosynthesis." Is the light of Christ shining brightly in your life? What is God growing in you? How are love, joy, peace, patience, kindness, goodness, faithfulness, gentleness, and self-control growing in your life?

- Remain in Jesus. Bear much fruit. Pray about it.

Day 5
Abide

My daughter recently picked some flowers out of the yard and gave them to me. She set them on the kitchen table "to keep them safe, Dad." The next day she found they had shriveled up. "What happened, Dad? Why did they die?" she asked. I explained how it's necessary for flowers to be connected to the plant, receiving water and nutrients. If the flower is removed from the plant, it soon dies. My daughter quickly decided to play with her dolls, but I had enjoyed this teachable moment.

Questions and Suggestions

- Read John 15:1–17. How will you stay connected to the vine this week? What fruit are you bearing for God in your life?

- Do you want more? Are you willing to be pruned by God? What might that look like for you? Pray about it.

Leading a Teenager to Christ

Throughout the year, natural times may come up to share the plan of salvation with your students. When that opportunity arises, you will want to be ready with a simple explanation told in a non-coercive manner. You may want to write it out or go over in your mind ahead of time what you will say. Following is a suggested plan and some related scriptures to spark your own prayerful thinking.

Share these thoughts in your own words:

1. God loves you and offers a wonderful plan for your life (John 3:16 and John 10:10).
2. Each of us has sinned and been separated from God, preventing us from knowing and experiencing God's plan (Romans 3:23 and Romans 6:23).
3. Jesus Christ is God's provision for our sin and separation from God (Romans 5:8 and John 14:6).
4. When we place our faith in Jesus Christ as Savior and Lord, then we can know and experience God's love and plan for our lives (John 1:12 and Ephesians 2:8–9).

Receiving Christ involves turning to God from self (repentance) and trusting Christ to come into our lives to forgive our sins and to make us what God wants us to be. It is not enough to agree to a list of facts about Jesus Christ or to have an emotional experience. We receive Jesus Christ by *faith,* as an act of the *will.*

If a student indicates that he or she is ready to make a decision, ask that person if he or she has any questions. If all seems clear, encourage the student to pray a prayer of repentance, asking God's forgiveness. You might guide the student with the following prayer:

God, I know I've done wrong and gone my own way. I am sorry. I want to follow you. I know Jesus died for my sins. I accept Jesus as my Savior and Lord. Thank you for forgiving me. Thank you for the gift of eternal life.

After the student has prayed, thank God for hearing his or her prayer, and affirm the student as a new Christian.

Explain to your student that as we pray, read the Bible, worship with other Christians, and tell others about what God has done for us, God will help us know how to live. Christ's presence is with us to help us live God's way. One step that a new believer should take is to be baptized. Baptism tells others that we are serious about following Jesus. Jesus set the example in being baptized and we are baptized to show that we are living for Jesus.

Talk to your pastor and your student's parents about his or her decision. Continue to encourage your student by giving him or her instruction and materials for setting up a daily devotional time. If possible, make arrangements with someone in the church to meet regularly with your student to act as a spiritual mentor.

There are a number of simple tract-type visuals to help you share Christ with your students:

- *It's Awesome!* (available at www.warnerpress.org or 800-741-7721)
- *Bridge to Life* (available at www.navpress.com)
- *The Answer* (available at www.studentdiscipleship.org)

EVALUATION FORM

Portrait of God

Community size: _____   Church size: _____   Class size: _____

Average preparation time: _____   Class length:_____

My class is made up of:_____ Sixth graders   _____ Ninth graders

_____ Seventh graders   _____ Tenth graders

_____ Eighth graders   _____ Eleventh graders

_____ Twelfth graders

Please rate the following on a scale of 1 (never) to 10 (always):

• Were the instructions clear and user-friendly?   _____

• Was the content challenging enough for students?   _____

• Were the activities adequate for this age level?   _____

• Did you use the Portable Sanctuaries? (Y/N)   _____

• Did you use the Digital Bridges CD? (Y/N)   _____

Which sessions and areas worked best for you? _____

_____

Which sessions and areas should be changed or improved?_____

_____

Suggestions and Comments:_____

_____

_____

_____

Your full name:_____

Congregation Name, City, and State: _____

Phone number (_____)_____   E-mail _____

--fold here--

--fold here--

NAME_____

ADDRESS_____

CITY/STATE/ZIP_____

* Don't forget your return address!

KEVIN STIFFLER, EDITOR
WARNER PRESS INC
PO BOX 2499
ANDERSON, IN 46018-2499

CPSIA information can be obtained
at www.ICGtesting.com
Printed in the USA
FFOW05n0634180116